A Home in Shalom'ville
The History of Asheville's Jewish Community

By Sharon C. Fahrer

Dedication

To our ancestors, whose hardships and successes have shaped our generation, as we will for those who follow and continue to tell our stories.

Contents

Forward

Sharon Fahrer was the first Jewish person I met in Asheville. In 2001, a friend of mine who was not Jewish, was hoping to convince me to move to Asheville. One of my concerns about moving to Western North Carolina was that there wouldn't be any Jews here. While I visited Asheville to look for a house, my friend brought me to a party in Montford, where she introduced me to Sharon. Little did I know at the time that this meeting would lead me into the embrace of the most warm and welcoming community of Jews I'd ever known – and ultimately into a career that focuses on keeping Jewish life in Asheville vibrant.

Soon after moving our family into the Montford neighborhood where I'd first met Sharon, my husband and I immediately joined the Asheville JCC. We spent our first summer in Asheville managing the grand opening of our own business – Sweet Heaven Ice Cream and Music Café – and flopping our exhausted bodies into the lounge chairs at the JCC pool for some much needed relaxation. We had no idea that we were following in the footsteps of so many other Jews that had moved to Asheville, started a business, and set out to raise a family in this peaceful and quirky town.

Sharon remained a friend and guide, helping us to navigate our new hometown. She introduced us to other young families, supported our fledgling business, and always seemed to have her finger on the pulse of what was happening in Asheville. I soon learned that Sharon was also a fascinating historian. Her work on the *Jewish Life in Western North Carolina* collection at UNC Asheville and T*he Family Store: A History of Jewish Businesses in Downtown Asheville, 1880-1990* is pretty remarkable. My Jewish pride and my connection to the Asheville Jewish community were deeply enriched by the wonderful exhibit of posters, featuring details about former Jewish business owners, that Sharon managed to get installed in store windows throughout downtown Asheville as part of *The Family Store* project.

My husband and I found it hard to support our household through our own little ice cream store. In spite of the stresses, I really enjoyed meeting lots and lots of people, including plenty of fellow Jews, who came to our shop. One of them was UNC Asheville professor, Sam Kaplan, who came up with the idea for the *Ice Cream Haggadah* that we collaborated on in 2003.

Sam also told me the joke: "How do you make a small fortune in Asheville? Bring a really big one." It was comforting to know we weren't the first entrepreneurs to find Asheville a challenging place to make a living! When you read about the history of Jewish Asheville featured in this book, however, you will learn that so many of our Jewish predecessors truly thrived in the numerous businesses and manufacturing enterprises they started here. They also became civic leaders and made significant contributions to both the Jewish community and all of Asheville – as Jewish Ashevillians continue to do today.

I now have the privilege of serving as the Executive Director of the Asheville JCC, and I am so proud to be a part of the wonderful history of Jewish Asheville. As we've celebrated the 75th anniversary of the JCC this year (2015), it's been incredibly fun to dig into the surprising history of Jews in Asheville. Sharon Fahrer was, of course, the first person we turned to when we saw this milestone on the near horizon. She had already begun working on the *Jewish Museum Without Walls*, a series of informational panels that are installed at institutions throughout Asheville, including at the JCC. Her idea for this book was the next logical step and a perfect tribute to honor the JCC's 75th year.

I hope you will enjoy reading about the many interesting characters that have shaped our community over the years. I also hope you will be as inspired as I am to continue building upon this strong tradition as we look to the future.

Lael Gray
Executive Director
Asheville Jewish Community Center

Proceeds from this publication benefit Asheville JCC programs. Books can be purchased at the JCC, 236 Charlotte Street or online at www.jcc-asheville.org

Second printing 2016

Published by History@Hand Publishing
333 Montford Avenue
Asheville, North Carolina 28801

Designed by KRT Design

Manufactured in the United States of America

ISBN 978-0-9746424-9-9

Library of Congress Control Number: 2015916803

On the Cover

1. Left to right across the top: Lewis Lipinsky, Coleman Zageir, Samuel Robinson, Morris Karpen, Sprinza Weizenblatt, Ernest Mills and Karl Straus

2. The Lewis Blomberg family in front of their Woodfin Street home, circa 1906. Left to right: Molly, Edna, Harry Frieda,?, Nat and Sigmund

3. Hilda Hoffman with a group of students in front of the original JCC building

4. The original JCC building on Charlotte Street

5. Celebration Israel held at Congregation Beth Israel (CBI) annually

6. Whiteside Mountain hike June 2, 1940, Leah Robinson Karpen and Michael Robinson.

Acknowledgements

It has truly taken a community to create this book from a pile of words. Jan Schochet started me on this journey, convincing me that Asheville's Jewish history needed to be documented. Lael Gray and Rochelle Reich took my crazy idea and ran with it, providing the support of the entire Asheville Jewish Community Center (JCC). Bebe Landis, Vic Fahrer and Lael Gray were the craftspeople who edited the raw material. Ross Terry of KRT Graphics has enhanced the photos that went into this book and created the design. In fact, he has been a patient friend throughout the process. I am eternally grateful to Leonard Rogoff for sharing his knowledge of North Carolina's Jewish history. He is my guru!

Important to the success of this publication are the dedicated people who work in our local archives. Helen Wykle, retired head archivist of the University of North Carolina-Asheville (UNC Asheville) D. Hiden Ramsey Library Special Collections (Ramsey Library Special Collections) was a huge inspiration. Gene Hyde, who succeeded Helen, and Colin Reeve are continuing that support and enthusiasm for our "Jewish Life in Western North Carolina" collection. Zoe Rhine, Ann Wright and their staff at the North Carolina Collection at Pack Memorial Library told me they would help in any way they could; and they did, answering questions and caring for the JCC collection as well as the materials of some of Asheville's Jewish business owners. They are all the keepers of our treasures.

The Center for Jewish Studies (CJS) at UNC Asheville, and especially Rick Chess its Director, has supported several of my Jewish history projects besides this book, including the Family Store and the Jewish Museum Without Walls as well as the archives at UNC Asheville.

True to the collaborative nature of our community, Rabbi Meiri of Congregation Beth HaTephila (CBHT), Rabbi Goldstein of Congregation Beth Israel (CBI) and Rabbi Susskind of The Chabad House of Asheville have all been encouraging of this project. Also thanks to those who contributed personal reminiscences and photographs, especially Jerry Sternberg, Leon Rocamora, Dennis Winner, Betty Golden, Sandy Slosman, Gene Winner, Skip and Lowell Pearlman, Bob and Audie Bayer, Phyllis Sultan, Harriet Winner, Barney Gradman, Natalie Shulimson Zeitlin and Ken Michalove among others.

Our Jewish community has an enormous wealth of talented and generous people. I realize someone may have been overlooked and welcome additional input so that all contributors to our community may be acknowledged. This is by no means the end of my research and archiving for future generations.

It is hoped that this book will encourage you to look at our collections as well as to look into your own family history. Donating material to an archive insures that it will be preserved and available to researchers and family members where ever they live.

Lastly, thank you for purchasing this book. You are supporting the JCC and its work in our community.

Sharon Fahrer

Asheville's Jewish Timeline

1860s .... First documented Jews in Asheville

1868-73 ...... Estimated period of delivery of *The Scattered Nation* by Zebulon Vance

1880 .... Railroad comes to Asheville; more Jews begin to arrive.

1880s .... Moses Cone becomes president of C.E. Graham Manufacturing

1891 .... Congregation Beth HaTephila founded

1892 .... Jewish section of Riverside Cemetery purchased

1899 .... Bikur Cholim synagogue formed

1902 .... Beth HaTephila purchases first building

1904 .... Solomon Schechter, head of the Jewish Theological Seminary, brought to Asheville to negotiate a merger of congregations

1905 .... **Jewish population of Asheville 100**

1907 .... Asheville has chapters of the National Council of Jewish Women

1908 .... Beth HaTephila joins Union of American Hebrew Congregations and becomes a reform congregation

1912 .... Asheville chapter of B'nai B'rith founded

1915 .... Young Men's Hebrew Association (YMHA) organized

1916 .... Mount Zion Jewish Cemetery organized by the West Asheville Hebrew Cemetery Association. Bikur Cholim's new building burns down. Another congregation, Anshei Yeshuran forms

1922 .... Agudas Israel, a reform congregation in Hendersonville, is founded

1924 .... Bikur Cholim building reconstruction completed

1926 .... Central Conference of American Rabbis holds annual meeting in Asheville

1927 .... **Jewish population of Asheville 700**

1928 .... B'nai B'rith erects monument to Vance in the "Westminster Abbey of the Southland" in Fletcher

1929 .... Thomas Wolfe's book *Look Homeward, Angel* published

1931 .... William Dudley Pelley, the would be American Hitler, moves to Asheville

1933 .... Black Mountain College founded

1933-45 ...... The Holocaust

1934 .... The first Brotherhood Day is observed

1935 .... Federated Charities organized; later becomes WNC Jewish Federation

1937 .... **Jewish population of Asheville 950**

1939 .... Jewish Community Relations Council organized in response to Kristallnacht.

1940 .... Jewish Community Center of Asheville opens on Charlotte Street

1947 .... **Jewish population of Asheville 600**

1949 .... Congregation Beth HaTephila erects a new building

1950 .... Bikur Cholim changes name to Beth Israel; Asheville has an active chapter of the National Council of Christians and Jews.

1960s .... Harry Winner helps integrate Asheville's retail sales force; Beth HaTephila has integrated Boy Scout troop. ASCORE works for racial integration (1960-65)

1960...........**Jewish population of Asheville 875**

1969...........Asheville Biltmore College becomes part of the University of North Carolina. Beth Israel moves into a new building

1970...........Connie Lerner the first Jewish American to be crowned Miss North Carolina

1970s..........Many businesses relocate from downtown to the new mall; family department stores close

1980...........**Jewish population of Asheville 1000**

1983...........Center for Jewish Studies created at UNC Asheville

1987...........Merger of Congregations Beth Israel and Beth HaTephila again discussed

1989...........Kenneth Michalove becomes Asheville's first Jewish mayor

1995...........Center for Diversity Education founded at the JCC

1997...........Leni Sitnik becomes Asheville's first female and second Jewish mayor

1997...........**Jewish population 1300**

2003............Hard Lox Jewish Heritage and Food Festival started

2005............Celebration Israel started

2006-2011 ..Maccabi Academy operated as a Jewish Day school

2006............The Chabad House of Asheville founded

2008............Jewish Film Festival started

2010............**3,400 people in Jewish-connected homes in WNC plus 835 seasonal residents**

2011............Jewish Family Services founded at JCC

2013............Esther Manheimer becomes Asheville's third Jewish mayor

2014............Jewish Secular Community of Asheville founded

Jewish merchants owned every business pictured in this section of Biltmore Avenue looking north toward Pack Square. 1924 (Courtesy of Ramsey Library Special Collections)

Old (about 1886) View of Court Square, Asheville. Looking Down Patton Ave. From Court House

This is the scene that greeted the early Jewish newcomers to Asheville in 1885. Pack Square looking toward Patton Avenue. (Pack Library North Carolina Collection)

There is a saying...

"Whenever the first Jew arrives, there is always a Jew there to greet him."

This was no doubt true in isolated, hard-to-reach Asheville. With the Buncombe Turnpike running through the center of town, and commerce spreading beyond the city's borders, Jewish peddlers and traders passed through the area. Harry Golden, a humorist and newspaper editor, noted, "Jews were trading with the eastern Cherokee who identified them as 'egg eaters' because, as observant Jews, they would not eat non-kosher meat." The first documented Jewish residents lived here in the 1860s. There was Levi Elias, who came to Asheville from Charleston, South Carolina to escape the upheaval of the Civil War and work in a local store. Also, a Mr. Hammerslough opened a general store, Hammersley and Company.

The Scattered Nation

With so few Jews in Asheville and the state of North Carolina, it is curious that Zebulon Baird Vance, Buncombe County native, two time Governor of North Carolina and a U.S. Senator, championed a bill in 1868 aimed at ending the ban on office-holding for non-Christians in the state legislature. Prior to 1868, the North Carolina constitution required a religious test that first limited the holders of public office to Protestants (1776) and later to Christians (1835). Vance later composed a Judeophilic speech, entitled *The Scattered Nation*, which was a rebuttal to those who voiced "objection to the Jew as a citizen." At a time when anti-Semitism was on the rise in America and Europe, Vance called for an "end to the restrictions placed on American Jews." He stated:

"…the Jew is what we have made him…Let us judge the Jew as we judge other men - by his merits. And above all let us cease the abominable injustice of holding the class responsible for the sins of the individual. We apply this to no other people."

This sentiment did not, however, include all Jews, mostly German Jews. Vance's acceptance of German Jews might have been due in part to his befriending Samuel Wittkowsky. This Prussian Jewish hatter offered the portly Vance a carriage ride to the train that would take him to Federal prison to serve his sentence with the other governors of the Confederacy after the Civil War. Vance and Wittkowsky became lifelong friends. Or, it might have been that Vance, like other Southerners of his time, was well versed in the Old Testament; and the speech was an expression of his biblical worldview.

Mrs. H.B. Haddon was an Asheville music teacher. She wrote "Vance's Grand March" in 1904. (Courtesy of the Special Collections Section, State Archives of North Carolina)

This speech was delivered in more than fifty towns and cities between 1874 and 1890 and reprinted in many newspapers. It became a missive of tolerance, and Vance became a hero to Jews. In 1897, a monument was erected in Asheville's Pack Square to honor Vance, the "local boy who made good." To Jews, it was a symbol of gratitude to Vance for elevating them to subjects of tolerance. This gratitude was not just felt by locals: in the early 1900s, New York department store (Macy's and Abraham and Straus) owner and philanthropist, Nathan Straus, laid a wreath in memory of Vance at Asheville's monument, donated $200 for its maintenance, and paid for an iron fence that separated the memorial from the public space on the square.

The 2015 restoration of the Vance monument has fueled arguments on honoring a man who was a white supremacist. Though some Jews, from Vance's time to the present, have considered *The Scattered Nation* speech as supporting Jews, scholars like Leonard Rogoff see the speech as "a truly embarrassing piece of 19th century romantic racialism." Rogoff describes it as a document that promotes Jews by denigrating African-Americans, and exalts German Jews at the expense of East European Jews. The debate will continue.

A Turning Point

During the 1870s, a few more Jews settled in Asheville. Solomon Whitlock, a Polish immigrant, and Solomon Lipinsky, born in Richmond, Virginia, arrived by stagecoach and opened businesses. Others came to Asheville in the 1880s, opened shops or worked in stores. Some peddled their merchandise and served as vital links to the mountains' rural economy, bringing goods and news to the isolated farmers. Often they were asked to answer questions or to bestow prayers from the *Hebrew Bible* as representatives of the "chosen people." When peddlers like S.H. Michalove saved enough capital, they opened stores in Asheville, and profited from their customer base that had been built on years of traversing the local countryside.

In 1880, the railroad came, linking Asheville to larger cities and larger markets. The population began to grow exponentially—from 2,610 in 1880 to 10,235 by 1890. Included in these numbers were enough Jews to start a congregation, Beth HaTephila (CBHT), in 1891.

Just why were so many people, Jews included, drawn to Asheville from the 1880s to the early 1900s? Three reasons emerge:

- **Economic opportunity**. The city was growing quickly and business opportunities were numerous. Immigrants followed the rail lines knowing they could find work in the expanding urban centers. North Carolina as a whole was becoming more urbanized and industrial. Mill "fever" had hit the state, and the mountains provided logging, mining, herb gathering and hydroelectric power. Jews opened stores to serve the increasing population.

- **Healing**. Doctors of the time were sending people with respiratory issues, such as tuberculosis, to the mountains to breathe clean air. Many sanatoriums were created here to accommodate them. People were also coming to the area to escape yellow fever, which was transmitted by the many mosquitoes of the low country. Wealthy and worldly people, like Gertrude Weil of Goldsboro, North Carolina, came for the hot springs and spas.

- **Natural beauty**. People who came here told friends and family about the beauty and fine accommodations in Asheville. Word spread and tourism became an industry!

Two Jews, Three Opinions

Members of Asheville's small Jewish community included Jews of diverse origins who brought their own religious practices and ideologies with them: Hammershlag (German); Elias (Sephardic—from Spain or Portugal); Lipinsky (Russian); Blombergs, Zagiers and Michaloves (Lithuanian),

and so on. Their diverse origins brought differing beliefs on what it meant to be a Jew. In order to fit into a southern community that was steeped in "fundamentalism, romantic religiosity, and high rates of church affiliation," they saw the necessity to meld their beliefs and form a Jewish "church" as a way to be accepted.

Being "strangers in a strange land," distant from established Jewish institutions, created another urgency to form a congregation. CBHT was founded as a conservative synagogue in an effort to compromise and appease its various factions. Since this pre-dated the formal organization of Conservative Judaism in America, its observances could be interpreted as an attempt to preserve some Jewish traditions but modernize others. An organ was purchased and a choir formed almost immediately, practices more accepted in the Reform movement.

Thus, it is not surprising that in 1899, some congregants, fearing that their current synagogue had strayed too far from Jewish tradition, formed an Orthodox synagogue, Bikur Cholim. Bikur Cholim translates as "visiting the sick," which suggests the group may have started as a welfare society to care for Jews who came to Asheville for their health. Synagogues were known to form welfare, burial (chevra kadisha) and welcoming (gemilut chasidim) societies early in their organizing period.

In the 1890s, it was not a certainty that Asheville's small Jewish population could support two congregations. At first, neither could even afford a full-time rabbi. However, by 1902, CBHT was able to purchase its first building, a former Baptist church on Spruce Street, across from the boarding house of Thomas Wolfe's mother Julia. It was in this neighborhood that Rebecca Rosenfeld, a Russian-born widow, ran a kosher boarding house that offered lodging to vacationers, as well as those seeking cures for their ailments. Oral history tells us that the thrifty Julia Wolfe would sometimes borrow food from Rebecca's establishment, knowing that she would not take Julia's non-kosher food in return!

In 1904, Solomon Schechter, head of the Jewish Theological Seminary in New York, was brought to Asheville to negotiate a merger of the two congregations. The merger did not succeed. This would not be the last time this debate would come up.

Both of Asheville's Jewish congregations struggled in their early years, especially CBHT. By the late 1910s, Asheville's Jewish population was 100. In 1907, the congregation had sixteen members and collected only $250 in dues, not enough money to support even a part-time rabbi. In 1908, after much discussion among its members, CBHT joined the Union of American Hebrew Congregations, becoming a Reform congregation.

For a short period in 1916, a small group split from Bikur Cholim to form a third congregation called Anshei Yeshuran. That year also saw the completion of a synagogue building for Bikur Cholim on Liberty Street, just a block from CBHT. Tragedy struck shortly before Rosh Hashanah that year, when the brand new Bikur Cholim synagogue mysteriously burned down. The rebuilt synagogue opened in 1924 on the silver anniversary of its congregation.

In 1919, CBHT again debated its religious affiliation, with some members wanting to join the Conservative movement. Solomon Lipinsky, owner of the Bon Marché department store and one of the congregation's founding members, gave a compelling speech for CBHT to remain Reform and won the vote.

Cemeteries

While it is necessary to have ten Jews for a minyan, it only takes one dead Jew to start a cemetery. It was important to establish early in the organization of a congregation, a place where Jews could be buried according to the customs and laws of their ancestors. And in Asheville, with so many people coming for health reasons, not all were fortunate enough to be cured and ultimately needed a place to rest for eternity. In 1891, CBHT debated whether to locate a cemetery in nearby Riverside Cemetery for $500, or further away in Chunns Cove for $250. Convenience won out, and the first Jewish cemetery was established within Asheville's Riverside Cemetery.

Bikur Cholim followed in 1916, organizing the West Asheville Hebrew Cemetery Association. Through financial aid, it provided free burial and funeral services for victims of tuberculosis in its Mount Zion Jewish Cemetery (MZJC). In 1951, the Board of Directors voted to change the name of the MZJC in West Asheville to Lou Pollock Memorial Park, in honor of a community volunteer. Pollock, a local shoe merchant, may hold the distinction of being the first living person to have a cemetery named after him.

CBHT Cemetery is within Riverside Cemetery in Montford. (Courtesy of Sharon Fahrer)

Health and Harry Finkelstein

Told he had malaria, Harry Finkelstein was one of the immigrants who came to Asheville for treatment. He soon found out that he had been misdiagnosed, but he liked it here and decided to stay. Harry and his four brothers each had a pawnshop in different cities in the South. To this day, there are still Finkelstein's Pawn Shops in Asheville and in Wilmington, North Carolina.

Harry Finkelstein 1878-1929 (Courtesy of Special Collections Belk Library and Information Commons Appalachian State University)

Thomas Wolfe immortalized Harry in *Look Homeward, Angel* as Saul Stein, pawnbroker. In Wolfe's short story, *Child by Tiger*, Harry is called Uncle Morris Teitlebaum and speaks broken English with a Yiddish accent: "Vell, vahat could I do? His moaney vas good!" The character is described as "bald headed, squat, with the face of an old monkey, displaying craggy nuggins of gold teeth." Not how most of us would want to be remembered, but perhaps a clue as to how locals viewed Jews during that time.

Wolfe's short story was based on a shootout in downtown Asheville in 1906 that left five people dead. As told by author and newspaper columnist Bob Terrill, a desperado named Will Harris went to the Gem Clothing store (owned by the Swartzberg family) on Patton Avenue, "Just steps from Pack Square." it read on their store front. Harris purchased some clothes, went around the corner to Finkelstein's Pawn Shop and bought a gun and ammunition. He then proceeded down South Main Street (now Biltmore Avenue) to a bar. He followed a woman home and took her hostage in her apartment. When her boyfriend came by, he realized what was happening and ran to alert the police. Harris then came out of the building and the shootout began, but Harris got away. A posse was formed, and some of its vigilantes borrowed guns from Finkelstein's Pawn Shop. Harry was proud to announce that, after they killed the criminal, all the borrowed guns were returned to his store!

In 1903, Harry opened Finkelstein's Pawn Shop. Nicknamed "The Poor Man's Bank," it served as the ATM of its time. Photo of Finkelstein's pawnshop on Pack Square 1960s (Courtesy of Ramsey Library Special Collections)

Beyond Asheville

Despite the distance from larger Jewish communities, Jews in Asheville were connected to current events in the Jewish world through newspapers, friends and relatives, and retailers returning from buying trips in New York or Baltimore. By 1907, Asheville could boast local chapters of the National Council of Jewish Women and the Zionist Society. In 1916, a Young Men's Hebrew Association was formed with fifty members, which, according to the *Asheville Citizen*, was intended "to improve…the young men of the Jewish race in Asheville and to advance their spiritual, physical and intellectual interests."

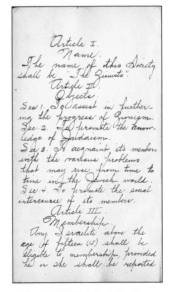

The bylaws of the Zionist Society 1906 (Courtesy of Ramsey Library Special Collections)

The 20s

The 1920s were a boom period for Asheville and North Carolina. Jews in general were joining the middle class and fitting more easily into American society. It was the era of Prohibition, but wine for Jews was exempt because it was part of their religious observance. The Ku Klux Klan launched a national campaign of "100 percent Americanism," railing against Catholics, African-Americans and Jews. Leonard Rapport, a member of the Blomberg family, observed the Klan in Asheville as "sort of bourgeois and socially acceptable." The KKK rented a space on College Street near Pack Square and actually invited Jews to join.

Jews were not mentioned in the local histories written by Forster Alexander Sondley in the 1920s and 1930s or in other major histories of that period. In regional cultural terms, Jewish people did not exist, remarked Patricia Beaver, a retired professor from Appalachian State University. Thomas Wolfe, writing during the same period, did not hesitate to include references to Jews in his writings, and it is clear that he interacted with Jews his whole life.

In 1926, the Central Conference of American Rabbis held its annual meeting in Asheville. Rabbi Moses Jacobson of CBHT proudly welcomed his colleagues, assuring them that Asheville was a "place of tolerance" with no race or religious prejudice. They laid a wreath at the Vance monument to show their appreciation to the city, and crafted a resolution extolling Vance as a "true American… who earned the love of all fair minded men." (*Asheville Citizen*, June 23, 1926) In fact, the *Asheville Citizen* reported conference proceedings and included relevant editorials. By 1927, Asheville had a population of 700 Jews, part of the 8,252 Jews living in North Carolina.

After the Conference, Jews started publicly honoring Vance. Another monument, sponsored by the B'nai B'rith, was erected in 1928 in the "Westminster Abbey of the Southland," on the grounds of Calvary Episcopal Church in Fletcher. This monument was one of many placed as a memorial to the "Lost Cause" (the Confederacy). Rabbi Stephen S. Wise, leader of the Free Synagogue in New York City, delivered its dedication speech before an estimated crowd of 2,000.

Members of the Jewish community attending a party at a house on Cumberland Avenue in the 1920s include: Lillian Rosenfeld, Beck Goldberger, Rabbi Elias Fox (sitting on a chair behind man sitting on the ground), Ms. Rose(?) Diamond, Dr. I. Mitchell Mann, Sol Bernstein (Sol Berney), Al Silverman, Nat Friedman (just below and next to man in front of the left column), Janette Feinstein, Izzie Goldstein, Hyman Goldberg, Harry and Fannie Finkelstein, Mark J. Kagan, Sender Argintar, Sophia Michalove, E. Jack Londow, Simon Argintar, Dora Blomberg, Dora Friedman, Louis Lichtenstein, Mr. and Mrs. Louis Sherman, Ann Rosenfeld, Tillie Schas, Max Markowitz, Ben Schas, Gus Lichtenfels (third man down from the left stair column in lighter suit) (Courtesy of Special Collections Belk Library and Information Commons Appalachian State University)

*Names are listed, but not located in the picture except as noted

The 30s

In December of 1930 Rabbi Elias Fox died from injuries sustained when he was hit by a car while crossing Merrimon Avenue. He was a Russian immigrant who had been the spiritual leader of Bikur Cholim for 25 years. The newspaper lauded him as one of the foremost leaders of the Jewish people in in WNC and said his close friends included hundreds of persons of other creeds. Interestingly he was involved in several civic organization including the Elks and the Masons (he had achieved the highest order, a 32nd degree Scottish Rite) and had a Masonic funeral.

The Great Depression had a huge impact on Asheville's Jewish community. The number of downtown Jewish businesses went from 145 (1915-1929) to 91 (1930-1944). Young Leon Rocamora Jr. was upset because he lost all of his $9.00 in savings when the bank failed. He had earned that money selling the perch he caught in Beaver Lake for five cents each. The reason he sold the fish was because his mother wouldn't let their family eat them! CBHT had to abandon plans for a new synagogue, and a house in Montford the congregation purchased as a Jewish center was foreclosed on. Membership dropped to fifty-four, and they could no longer afford Rabbi Jacobson, even though he cut his salary. Because they could no longer pay him a living wage, he retired, having served from 1922 to 1934. It is interesting to note that the Rabbi was a vehement anti-Zionist. He thought too much effort was spent on promoting a Jewish state, and that this was taking energy away from the American Reform movement. Despite his opinion, Asheville had a Zionist Organization of America chapter with 122 members by 1944.

Two members of the Jewish community, Jules Levitch and attorney Alvin Kurtus, worked with the cooperation of the Buncombe County Sheriff to have Pelley charged with securities fraud in 1935. (Courtesy of Ramsey Library Special Collections)

Asheville was not immune from the Nazi threat. This decade saw the arrival of William Dudley Pelley, a virulent anti-Semite and Nazi sympathizer. He led his Silver Shirt League to Asheville in 1932, published a weekly paper, *The Liberator*, in Biltmore Village, and started Galahad College in the Asheville Club for Women on the corner of Charlotte Street and Sunset Parkway (it did not last long). Rabbi Jacobson, in his 1933 Purim sermon, warned that although the Jews as a body were respected, they did face danger with the rise of Hitler in Germany and the presence of Pelley. To Asheville's credit, Pelley had few local followers. Sidney Schochet, a downtown business owner, remembered that Pelley always had three or four "athletic looking guys" accompanying him when he walked down the street. In 1941, Pelley relocated to Noblesville, Indiana. There, he was arrested and jailed for sedition and insurrection.

To strengthen the bond of interfaith communities (and possibly to counteract Pelley's notoriety), the first Brotherhood Day was observed in 1934. Concern for the area's image—particularly to tourists —may have been a major factor in gentile Asheville's collaboration with its Jewish community. The local Brotherhood Day ceremony was supported by the National Conference of Christians and Jews, whose aim was to link the "ideal of religious tolerance to Americanism," according to Seth Epstein. By the late 1930s, the spirit of tolerance had gained so much momentum, the B'nai B'rith and the United Daughters of the Confederacy held joint ceremonies memorializing Vance on his birthday at the monument in Pack Square.

The 1930s also saw the founding of Black Mountain College offering progressive education in the nearby town of Black Mountain. Hitler had closed the Bauhaus school of design in Germany; and some of its faculty, including Josef and Anni Albers, came to this small town in North Carolina. Coming to America to teach at a university was a way to escape Nazi Germany. The school attracted many talented Jews, such as artist Ben Shahn, photographer Aaron Siskind, poet Paul Goodman, novelist Isaac Rosenfeld, literary critic Alfred Kazin and Albert Einstein (who lectured there). They had many public performances, which local citizens were welcome to attend, thus bringing a taste of European culture to the area.

During this period, Rabbis Alexander Kline and Robert Jacobs of CBHT represented Asheville's Jews in various civic organizations. In 1935, Rabbi Kline began giving a weekly radio address on WWNC called *Message of Israel*, which was continued by Rabbi Jacobs beginning in 1939. Carrying civic involvement a step further, Rabbi Jacobs became the Chairman of the Public Relations Committee for the Community Chest (the predecessor of the United Way).

As a way to unite different factions of Judaism, new, non-affiliated organizations would be formed. Chapters of Hadassah, the Ladies Auxiliary, Jewish Book Club, Young Judea and the North Carolina Association of Jewish Women met regularly. The Western North Carolina Jewish Federation started in 1935 as Federated Charities. Sarah Goldstein, the first secretary, recalled that in its first year, Federated Charities raised $3,000 and "we thought we were wonderful!" This was a very organized community.

In 1939, in response to Kristallnacht, a Jewish Community Relations Council (JCRC) was organized as part of the structure of Federated Charities. Its purpose was to build Jewish political and economic influence in Asheville. However, CBHT, not wanting to take a political stand, did not participate. The rationale was that Reform Judaism was a religious brotherhood, not an organization of persons seeking political and economic favors from the general population.

After a decline, CBHT's membership grew again at the end of the decade—from 73 members in 1938, to 113 in 1941—as more Jews affiliated in the shadow of the Holocaust. In fact, Asheville's Jewish population grew to 950 in 1937. And in that year, Asheville had the largest Jewish population in North Carolina, despite Charlotte having twice the population.

And Now a Center for the Jewish Community

Even as Asheville's Jews found social acceptance, there were still anti-Semitic undertones. Jews in Asheville were not able to purchase homes in certain neighborhoods or join local country clubs or social organizations. Though they participated in civic organizations, they often remained social outsiders. This led to founding parallel organizations. The Jewish Community Center (JCC) began organizing in 1939 and was officially chartered in 1940. It came to serve as the social nucleus of the Jewish community.

As non-Jewish teens' social lives revolved around their church youth groups, Jewish teens turned to a B'nai B'rith national youth organization known as AZA. Dennis Winner, a native Ashevillian whose father owned Winner's Department Store, recalled:

> "The Jewish youth of Asheville from both synagogues were, for the most part, pretty close to each other. We kept together through our membership in the B'nai B'rith Youth Organization."

AZA had social events with Jewish youth from all across North Carolina and the Southeast. For those from rural areas, this was an opportunity to meet other Jewish youth. Their mothers belonged to Sisterhoods and Hadassah, and their fathers, Brotherhoods or B'nai B'rith. They supported Jewish causes through the Federated Jewish Charities.

Kerry Friedman, who grew up going to the JCC, pointed out that the JCC's preschool and swimming pool were open to non-Jews, and this became a way to combat anti-Semitism on a person-to-person basis. As Jonathan Sarna, a professor of American Jewish history at Brandeis University has written:

"When we have friends who are members of a persecuted group, we look at that group differently. You don't listen to folks who make broad unsavory accusations because you say 'My friend is not like that.'"

Aleph Zadik Aleph (AZA) Convention at CBHT 1963 (Courtesy of Ramsey Library Special Collections)

Jewish Revival: The 40s and 50s

Rabbi David Wachtfogel of Bikur Cholim spoke at the Vance memorial ceremony in 1941. He characterized Vance as a model for the principles and ideals we were fighting for in World War II, including "justice, truth, liberty and freedom for all." (*Asheville Times*, May 13, 1941) Before the war, Karl Straus and Fred Hoffman left Europe and arrived in Asheville, helped by relatives to resettle. After the war, Fred brought his wife, Hilde, here to start a new life. Later, other survivors of the Holocaust made their way to Asheville, including Walter Ziffer, Miriam Rudow, Harry and Lily Lerner, Ilse Hyman, Lotte Meyerson, Rubin Feldstein and Irma Cantor. Some of their stories are documented in *Choosing to Remember: From the Shoah to the Mountains (Shoah - Survivors and Witnesses in Western North Carolina)*, a project of the Center for Diversity Education at UNC Asheville. Soldiers returning or resettling after World War II opened businesses such as the Vanderbilt Shirt Factory. They started families, and Asheville's Jewish population began to increase.

Anti-Semitism worldwide in the 1930s made Jews, even in Asheville, feel less safe. Jerry Sternberg, whose family arrived in Asheville around 1900, recalled that when Jewish organizations would meet in public buildings such as the S&W Cafeteria, a guard would be posted outside the door. This insecurity led to the founding of the JCC as a gathering place where Jews could feel more comfortable. The interior of the S&W Cafeteria (Courtesy of Ramsey Library Special Collections)

Rabbi Sidney Unger took over the pulpit of CBHT in 1946 and became Asheville's Jewish spokesperson for tolerance. He moderated small-scale discussions at the JCC for the Jewish Youth League and was involved in many civic organizations. The Rabbi moderated a town meeting radio program that brought together many of Asheville's whites-only organizations (which included Jewish organizations) to discuss political and social issues.

During Rabbi Unger's tenure, CBHT was a classical Reform congregation. According to the Jewish Virtual Library:

> *"Classical Reform was the type of Reform Judaism that developed in the late 19th century. American Jews, most of whom were of central European background, saw the tremendous influence that liberal religion had on their Protestant neighbors and wanted to develop a form of Judaism equivalent to Episcopalianism, Presbyterianism, and, especially, Unitarianism."*

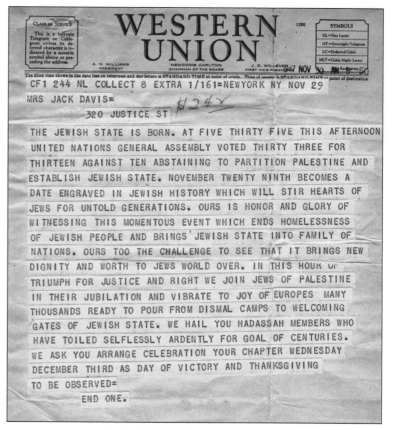

Announcement of the Creation of the State of Israel (Courtesy of Ramsey Library Special Collections)

Most of the temple's service was in English, with an organ and choir. Certain traditions, such as keeping kosher, were not observed. In fact, when Rabbi Unger came to Asheville, the Sunday schools of the synagogue and the temple were combined and met at the JCC. Rabbi Unger objected because the children wore yarmulkes, so he disbanded the combined school.

The conclusion of World War II and the brutality of the Holocaust influenced the outlook of all Jews. Rabbi Unger insisted CBHT move forward and fulfill its dream for a new building. When the synagogue was completed in 1949, its International Modernism design exemplified the resolve to look toward the future with pride and self-determination. A prominent Asheville architectural firm, Six Associates created the plans. Many of Asheville's civic and religious leaders spoke at the dedication ceremony, which was broadcast over the radio.

Asheville's downtown was still a destination where many customers came to shop for their necessities. A large proportion of Asheville's Jews continued to run retail businesses there. Many of the shop owners were now the children of the founders, or sometimes shop owners' children established new businesses. This second generation of Asheville Jews was more assimilated than their parents had been.

Bikur Cholim had its own challenges. Between 1940 and 1953, the congregation had seven different rabbis. Most were Orthodox and had a hard time adjusting to life in a small Southern town. As an American-born generation took over congregation leadership, they moved away from more Orthodox practices and joined the Conservative Movement, affiliating with the United Synagogue of America. In 1950, Bikur Cholim became Congregation Beth Israel (CBI). During the 1950s, the members voted to shorten the Saturday service and adjust the start

Beth HaTephila synagogue building 1902-1949 (Courtesy of Ramsey Library Special Collections)

time from 10 a.m. to 8 a.m. so members could open their businesses on the busiest shopping day of the week. This change reflected the compromises Jewish shop owners had to make in order to maintain their Jewishness and their livelihood.

In 1969, the congregation moved from Liberty Street into its current building on Murdock Street.

St. Genevieve of the Pines and Girls' Education

St. Genevieve of the Pines (SGP) was founded in 1913, having as one of its goals to raise the expectations of female students. Mother Margaret Potts, the principal of the school and subsequently Mother Superior of the Order, wrote:

"We wanted to develop character and help each individual student through learning and moral guidance to find fulfillment and grow into a worthwhile person."

While the campus atmosphere was essentially religious, there was limited emphasis on Catholicism. In fact, the school population was generally 25% Catholic, 25% Jewish and 50% other (Protestant denominations, Greek Orthodox, etc.). Elaine Scagnelli (born Fitch) was a student at SGP who became a teacher and a nun there. She recalls:

"The Jewish community in Asheville was very supportive and mostly sent their children to SGP and Gibbons Hall instead of to other private schools in the area. The sisters were very grateful for the support of the families of non-Catholics. We were very careful not to say anything negative about religions that were not Catholic, and Protestants and Jews were not required to take Catholic instruction. We believed in encouraging students to take their religion seriously whatever it was."

The Academy took a holistic approach to student development that included education of body, intellect and will. Their goal was to teach youth how to think, to study and to judge. According to Jan Schochet, SGP alum, Mother Potts could empathize with the Jewish experience of intolerance and prejudice, having grown up in the only Catholic family in a small Tennessee town. Jan observed that SGP was:

"the best school in the area. Therefore, Jewish parents wanted to send their kids there if they could afford it. Plus, for some I'm sure, it was a 'status' thing—to be in a place that cost more money, where you could rub elbows with the rich."

Jewish parents also participated in school organizations. Lowell Pearlman remembers his mother, Anne Pearlman, served as President of the parents organization when he attended Gibbons Hall in the 1950s.

According to Brenda Lilly, a graduate of SGP, the school emphasized the importance of education and pursuing your dream. Brenda created a television show, "State of Grace," based on her experience as a Catholic student whose best friend was Jewish. In real life, her friend was Connie Lerner, the future Miss North Carolina, whom Brenda says played the Virgin Mary every year in the Christmas pageant. (Jan was given the part of Joseph in school plays because she was the tallest!) The series, which aired on Fox from 2001-2003, received many awards, including The Parents Television Council, the Humanitas Award and a Jewish Image Award.

African-American Relations

After the Civil War, African-Americans worked mostly in domestic occupations and in the service sector. For decades, the North Carolina culture was dominated by a white majority in a society that promoted racism as an ordinary way of life. During the years of Jim Crow segregation, many Jews had a different relationship with African-Americans than other Southern whites in the community. Jews knew African-Americans as customers, employees or tenants. Jewish businesses often catered to African-American customers, allowing them to try on clothing when other white shopkeepers would not, and extending them credit.

Asheville City Directories list Jewish-owned businesses on Eagle Street, part of "The Block" (Eagle and Market Street), which was the African-American shopping district. In 1900, Isaac and Rebecca Michalove ran a grocery on the corner of Eagle and Valley Streets and lived above their store. By 1928, eight Jewish-owned businesses were listed on Eagle Street, including four groceries, used furniture, second hand clothing, men's furnishings and women's clothing stores. During the 1930s, Jewish professionals, including Dr. Samuel Robinson (an optometrist and father to Leah Karpen and Rabbi Michael Robinson) and Dr. Sprinza Weizenblatt (an ophthalmologist), treated African-American patients with respect and equality. Rabbi Robinson recalled that his father addressed his African-American patients as "Mr." and "Mrs." to the disapproval of his receptionist. At the age of ten, Michael sat in the back of the bus with his nanny.

Jewish households often hired African-American maids. Marilyn Patton kept a picture of her longtime housekeeper in a frame alongside her other family photos. Some African-American cooks learned Yiddish and made favorite recipes, like matzo balls and tzimmis, as well as Jewish holiday specialties.

Even during the depths of the Depression, Jews hired African-Americans when others refused to do so. Harry Blomberg, owner of a General Motors dealership (today known as Harry's On The Hill), was criticized for hiring a black auto mechanic, John Baxter. Before being hired by Harry, Baxter had gone to New York, where he learned to be a transmission mechanic. When he came home to Asheville, Baxter opened his own business which was unsuccessful because he could not find skilled workers, so he went to work for Harry.

Jews were not immune to perpetuating the racist norms of the time. Blackface minstrel shows were a popular form of entertainment in synagogues, and Asheville was no exception. This is a photo of a party at the home of Harry Finkelstein 167 Broadway, 1920s. *Lillian Rosenfeld, Ms. Novick (sister of Bess Swartzberg), Dora and Ben Schas, Roy and Bess Swartsberg, Freda and Dora Blomberg, Janette Feinstein, E. Jack Londow (son of Rabbi Londow), Tillie Schas, Esther Kroman (later Mrs. Samuel Robinson) (sixth from right in back row), Simon (back row fifth from right) and Sender Argintar (back row top hat), Nat Friedman (left of Sender), Izzie Goldstein, Harry and Fannie Finkelstein, Beck Goldberg, Dora Landow (sister of Jack), Dora Littman, Ms. Littman, Dr. I Mitchell Mann, Ben Pollock (second from right on the floor) Jack Blomberg (fourth from right on the floor), Abe Kantrowitz (Kanter)(on floor very right) (Courtesy of Special Collections Belk Library and Information Commons Appalachian State University)

*Names are listed, but not located in the picture except as noted

Dr. Patricia Beaver of Appalachian State University remembered that after giving a talk on African-American and Jewish relations at the JCC in 1995:

"An elderly black gentleman rose and addressed the gathering. In an eloquent personal testimony, he thanked the Jewish community for their support of the black community. He related that when he was young, he found employment at the Jewish Community Center, and had worked for individuals in the congregation. This employment was critical to his family's survival, particularly during the Depression; but more than that, he had always been treated with dignity and respect."

(The gentleman was probably referring to working at one of the synagogues and not the JCC, as it was not in existence during the Depression.) His statement is a reminder that the Jewish and the African-American communities had social and economic connections, which helped them both survive.

The Investors Club was the "Who's Who" of CBHT. Several of its members became CBHT presidents. They would hire a bus and take annual trips. Left to right: Larry and Sylvia Mills, Marty and Nina Cooper Gross, Karl and Sylvia Straus, Ernie and Albina Mills, Leon and Dot Rocamora, Bernie and Mildred Gordon, Leo and Sylvia Finkelstein. Gene and Elaine Fater Shapiro, Sy and Dorothy Fligel, Norman and Phyllis Sultan. Missing from the picture are William and Joan Rocamora, Fred and Anne Pearlman and David and Audrey Pearlman (Courtesy of Phyllis Sultan)

The 60s

The 1960s saw a lot of changes in America: civil rights, the Vietnam War, the Beatles, and for Jews, some social barriers began to break down.

Civil Rights

While the history of discrimination made most Jews sympathetic to the plight of African Americans, it also made Jews throughout the South fearful of open participation in the civil rights movement. As an act of self-preservation, Jews adapted to the laws and customs of their adopted homeland. In the American South, that meant accepting racial segregation. Fear of anti-Semitic reprisal was foremost in the minds of many southern Jews who might have been tempted to openly champion the cause of civil rights. This was also true in Asheville, where some remembered the presence of William Pelley and his Silver Shirts. Some were also afraid they would lose customers and their livelihood. In 1955, Herbert Wadopian wrote a letter to James Stokely, thanking him for writing a letter to the editor of the newspaper rebuffing a Dr. Bell (father-in-law of Evangelist Billy Graham). Wadopian found Bell's comments to be racist, but was reluctant to reply because he was himself a member of a minority group and felt it would sound better if the responding letter came from someone of Dr. Bell's own faith.

Nonetheless, members of the Jewish community worked quietly to make changes even before the civil rights movement of the 1960s. According to Al Whitesides, a member of ASCORE (Asheville Student Committee on Racial Equality), the Jewish community contributed funds to their group of students from the all black Stephens-Lee High School. This enabled them to advance racial integration in the city.

When Harry Winner opened Winner's Department Store in the 1940s, he removed the separate colored and white water fountains, replacing them with one modern electric ice water machine. Later, Harry, who was born and raised in Savannah, Georgia, felt it was time for African-Americans to have better paying and more visible jobs than just being janitors and elevator operators. In the 60s, he asked a second-generation elevator operator if she would become a sales clerk. He then went to other

Harry and Julienne Marder Winner (Courtesy of Leslie Winner)

Harry Winner was the first white business owner in Asheville to place an African-American fashion manikin in his window. Winner's Department Store on Haywood Street (Courtesy of Leslie Winner)

department stores and convinced their managements to also place African-Americans in sales positions on the same day, thus avoiding boycotts. After the store's janitor died suddenly, Harry called the man's high school-aged son, Herb Watts, into his office. Harry knew that the family depended on the older Watts' wages, and so he offered to pay Herb his father's salary if he would work after school and on Saturdays.

Harry's son Dennis remembered that, during the 1950s, the city had an active chapter of the National Conference of Christians and Jews. Each year, there were three chairmen, one each from the Jewish, Protestant and Catholic communities. The organization's main function was to put on Brotherhood Week every February. During one of the years that Harry Winner was the Jewish chairperson, the Brotherhood Week banquet was to be held at the old George Vanderbilt Hotel (now the Vanderbilt Apartments) on Haywood Street. The entertainment for the banquet was to be a concert by several African-American church choirs. However, the hotel was segregated and refused to allow African-American participants on the premises to perform. Harry, incensed over this, convinced the other chairmen to move the banquet to a local African-American church.

During the 1960s, Dr. Samuel Robinson worked tirelessly to integrate the Daniel Boone Boy Scout Council and its camp. His son, Michael, grew up in Asheville, became a Rabbi and had a pulpit in New York. Michael became active in the civil rights movement and was arrested during a demonstration in Florida. Dr. Robinson only found out about the arrest when he went to E.C. Goldberg's newsstand on Patton Avenue and saw his son's picture on the front page of *The New York Times*. A local Florida rabbi remarked that Northern rabbis should keep their noses out of Southern civil rights issues. Rabbi Robinson pointed out he was Southern, a native of Asheville.

As attitudes changed, Jewish people gradually began to feel freer to openly support African-American equality:

- Sometime in 1967-68, CBHT started the first integrated Boy Scout troop in Asheville. Its second scoutmaster was Jasper Dunlap, who was the Temple janitor at the time.

- During the 1960s, the Wolfsons, a Jewish family from Florida, owned WLOS-TV. Their news commentator was Mort Cohn, a member of CBHT. He spoke out on behalf of peaceful integration during those years.

- By 1969, attitudes had changed enough that Dr. Robinson felt free to write a letter to the editors of the *Citizen-Times* supporting the cessation of racial hatred.

- Leslie Winner, daughter of Harry Winner, became one of the most important civil rights lawyers in North Carolina.

The 70s and 80s

In the 1970s, with the spread of suburban malls, Asheville's downtown died as many businesses moved out or closed up, including Bon Marché and Winner's. The era of the family-owned department store was over. The Man Store, owned by Coleman Zageir, was swallowed up by Hart Schaffner & Marx and moved to a mall. Local clothing manufacturers also went out of business as the textile industry moved overseas or the owners sold their businesses or retired. These included Hadley Cashmere owned by Richard and Jane Haber, Connie Fashions owned by Harry and Lily Lerner, Mars Manufacturing owned by Robert Bayer, and the Vanderbilt Shirt Company owned by Milton Lurey, Herman Silver and Herbert Wadopian. Tops for Shoes, owned by the Carr family, was one of the few Jewish stores that remained in business downtown, surviving because of their large selection of shoe sizes and their great customer service.

Asheville's Jewish residents were as always very active in civic affairs. In 1979 Fred Pearlman was the only Jewish Chairman of the Board of a YMCA in the United States. Throughout his career he also had held leadership roles in the Asheville Civitan Club, Water Commission, Alcoholic Beverage Control Board and the Chamber of Commerce as well as the United Jewish Appeal. His wife Anne was President of Asheville Community Theatre.

Many of the business owners' children went off to college and settled in larger cities where they found more job opportunities. Instead of going into retail like their parents, many Jews raised in Asheville became professionals in their new cities.

The Center for Jewish Studies (CJS) at the University of North Carolina-Asheville was created in 1983. It connected the local Jewish community to the University, introducing a variety of courses related to Jewish studies and bringing modern scholars to speak and teach.

In 1987, a merger between CBHT and CBI was again discussed, as synagogue and temple memberships had declined. The idea was rejected, as consensus could not be reached on the definition of "Who is a Jew?" While this question pivots on the requirement that Jewish heritage passes through the mother, Reform Jews believe that either parent can qualify their children's Jewishness.

Kenneth Michalove became Asheville's first Jewish Mayor in 1989 and served until 1993. This demonstrated that it was not just the Jewish community that supported him, but also the community at large.

The 90s

The 1990s saw the reinvention of Asheville's downtown as a destination of arts and entertainment. The city again began to grow and thrive, this time attracting many retirees and new families to its Jewish community. While downtown Asheville experienced this resurgence with many locally owned shops and restaurants, the days of Jewish retail dominance had disappeared. Nevertheless, Jews continued to be influential. Jewish entrepreneurs opened restaurants, became real-estate developers or realtors, and opened professional offices. Leni Sitnik became Asheville's first woman mayor and the second Jewish mayor, serving from 1997 until 2000.

Deborah Miles recalls that the Jewish Community Relations Council (JCRC) was actively working on school issues. Concerns included scheduling sporting meets and exams on Jewish holidays. The JCRC also sponsored a discussion about hate groups in the area, led by staff members of the Anti-Defamation League. The Center for Diversity Education (now named the Center for Diversity Education at UNC Asheville) was founded at the JCC in 1995 to raise awareness and teach social justice skills in the community.

Into The New Century

The Asheville Jewish community has grown tremendously since the turn of the century, as Jews from all over the country have been drawn to Asheville's lifestyle, with its natural beauty and rustic cosmopolitanism. This influx of Jews has brought new ideas and perspectives to the community. Asheville's Jewish population grew from 600 people in 1947 to 1,300 people in 1997. Since then, the area's Jewish community has more than doubled, reaching an estimated 3,400 year-round residents and 835 part-timers in Buncombe County in 2010, according to a Brandeis University study. (Asheville's population was not broken out of the study.)

Jewish Family Services, founded at the JCC, became an independent agency in 2012. With the addition of the Chabad House of Asheville in 2006 and the Jewish Secular Community of Asheville (JSCA) in 2014, there are even more opportunities to remain "Jewishly connected." The JCC, which celebrated its 75th Anniversary in 2015, is bursting at the seams and is about to expand.

At a time when many southern Jewish communities are shrinking, Asheville's welcoming Jewish community has never had more members and continues to grow, as Jews are drawn to the eclectic charms of the city. As Asheville thrives, so does its Jewish community pointing toward an even brighter future.

Annual events

Popular annual events sponsored by one organization and attended by the entire community include: the Hard Lox Jewish Food and Heritage Festival (October), Chanukah Live, the Asheville Jewish Film Festival (April or May), Celebration Israel (Israeli Independence Day), the Purim Festival, Yom Ha Shoah, Holocaust Memorial Day (a week after Passover ends), and the Falafel 5k (Spring). Bi-annual parties around town and a bi-annual gala are sponsored by the JCC.

Happy kids create light at The Chabad House of Asheville's "Chanukah Live" celebration in 2013. (Courtesy of The Chabad House Asheville)

Lighting the Menorah at Chanukah Live. Left to right: Jay Jacoby, Brad Morris, Lael Gray, Alison Gilreath, Ed Fidelman, Judi Goloff, Nadine Fidelman, Rabbi Susskind (Courtesy of The Chabad House Asheville)

Today's Asheville

We continue to be a community of diverse opinions, embracing many ideals. As Rabbi Cohen of Bikur Cholim once said,

"We can live with differences, disagreements and debates; they do not have to descend into conflict. Our mission is to work toward unity and integration."

While some subjects will never foster consensus among Jews, such as Israel, American politics, or even how to observe Jewish traditions, we have learned to amicably "agree to disagree." Our community is strong because we *do* have choices, and our small numbers keep us united as one community. Asheville's Jewish history has laid the foundation for each of its members to be who they are today.

Old-timers who knew the stories and witnessed events of the past are passing on. Our senior community members have been through some of the best times and some of the worst times in modern Jewish history. Yet Jews continue to find a welcoming home here. Asheville has a growing and diverse community that supports Jewish values and beliefs. Jews' deep roots here help to provide a sense of comfort, security and familiarity that makes us all feel like we belong.

CBHT hired its first woman rabbi, Batsheva Meiri, in 2008 and renovated and added on to its synagogue. Its membership grew from 130 families in 1985 to 280 in 2015. Rabbi Meiri inspires her congregants to connect spiritually and intellectually with their Judaism and continue to practice Tikkun Olam (healing the world) (Courtesy of Laurie Johnson Photography)

In 2014, CBI brought vibrant, young Rabbi Justin Goldstein to serve its 180 families. His congregants see him as a dynamic leader, gifted teacher and connector of people (Courtesy of Rabbi Justin Goldstein)

Rabbi Shaya and his wife Chana Susskind established The Chabad House of Asheville in 2006. Due to their warm and embracing personalities and Chana's cooking, The Chabad House of Asheville celebrated its 10th anniversary in 2015. (Courtesy of The Chabad House Asheville)

Lael Gray, Executive Director of the JCC, has a background in business management, communications and community activism. She held a variety of positions at the JCC, from bus driver to Children's Program Director since 2003 (Photo courtesy of Laurie Johnson Photography)

IN THE BEGINNING...

In 1891, Asheville was a small town of 10,000 people, with a handful of Jewish residents. That year 27, men met at the Lyceum Hall on South Main Street, now Biltmore Avenue, to perpetuate "the age-old Jewish responsibility for the care and education of their children, the establishment of a house of worship and the conduct of services, and the creation of a meeting place for good fellowship." Their goals also included: purchasing a cemetery, acquiring a building or accomplishing "any other purpose within the scope of Judaism." The organization was named Congregation Beth Ha Tephila (CBHT), the House of Prayer, and affiliated with the Conservative movement. Land for a cemetery was purchased in nearby Riverside Cemetery by 1892.

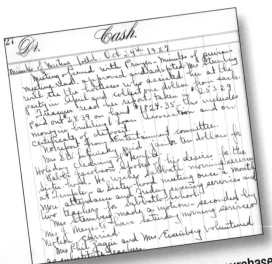

The same year the congregation purchased their building, in 1902, the women of the congregation formed The Jewish Ladies Aid Society to help pay for the building. They also took responsibility for care of the cemetery, made burial shrouds and visited the sick. The group affiliated with the National Federation of Temple Sisterhoods in 1922.

In 1930, a Men's club was organized as part of the National Federation of Temple Brotherhoods. Pictured is the 1975-1976 Brotherhood Retreat at Harry Blomberg's summer home on Lake Lure, the discussion topic was Massada.

Front Row: Harry Blomberg, Rabbi Funston, Stan Frumpkin, Dr. Albert Kodack. Middle Row: Arnie Sgan, George Pozner, Dr. Stan Marks, Emmanuel Newman, Gaston (Gerry) Haller, Dr. Larry Rapoport.

Back Row: Earl Schrier, Ed Wolfe, Ike Chicurel, Charles Grand, Charles Brewer, ?.

This chapter is an interpretive panel located at:
43 N Liberty St, Asheville, NC 28801
Phone: (828) 253-4911
www.bethhatephila.org

Initially the congregation met in old Lyceum Hall on South Main Street (now Biltmore Avenue). In April of 1902 they purchased the former First Baptist Church Erected in 1863, it had been sold to the Christian Church in 1891 and given to a Reverend T.M. Meyers in lieu of his salary. He had been forced to mortgage the property and was glad to sell it to CBHT for $2000. In 1908 the congregation joined the Union of American Hebrew Congregations and the Reform movement. The final service in the Spruce Street temple was August 12, 1949.

Dr. Julian Morganstern on the left and Rabbi Sydney Unger on the right on the occasion of the laying of the cornerstone of Congregation Beth Ha Tephila, October 20, 1948.

The new temple building (pictured) was dedicated on August 19, 1949. Two prominent figures in the Reform movement participated: Dr. Jacob Rader Marcus, president of the Central Conference of American Rabbis and founder of the American Jewish Archives and Dr. Julian Morgenstern, President Emeritus of Hebrew Union College. Joseph Dave and Sydney Wein were the building committee co-chairs.

Rabbi Sidney E. Unger (1896-1972) was a strong personality who was involved in many civic organizations in the greater Asheville community. "Hear O Israel," his Saturday night radio show, broadcast over WWNC, offered educational programs for Christian clergy and laity in order to establish a dialogue between the Jewish and Christian communities of Asheville. Photo: Rabbi Unger moderating Asheville's "Town Meeting of the Air" on WNCA radio which was later taken over by WLOS.

CONGREGATION
Beth HaTephila

Rabbis

The Rabbis of CBHT serve not only as its spiritual leaders, but as representatives of the Jewish people to the larger Asheville community. Among the most outstanding of those were Rabbi Moses P. Jacobson (1922-1934), Rabbi Sydney E. Unger (1946-1965) and Rabbi Robert Ratner (1992-2007). Rabbi Jacobson advocated the return of Jewry to the synagogue as a center for Jewish life. "He stirred a passion of Love for Judaism," said member Dr. Samuel Robinson. In 1934 he joined with clergy of other faiths for the first Brotherhood Day program in Asheville. Brotherhood Day was a show of unity that may have been a response to William Dudley Pelley, the would be American Hitler, who moved to Asheville claiming the vortex drew him here. Rabbi Unger came to CBHT at the urging of his lifelong friend, Joseph Dave. He recognized that for 25 years, people had hoped to see a new temple built, and plunged into the endeavor. He said, "You got me here to be your Rabbi. Give me the tools to work with." During his tenure the religious school was also constructed. Rabbi Ratner helped revitalize the temple at a time when membership was low. (Asheville was not yet "cool" when he came so there were few new people joining.) In fact his six children doubled the enrollment of the religious school!

September 1959 heralded the completion of the dream of CBHT founders with the dedication of a new school building. The congregation now had a House of Worship, a House of Assembly, and a House of Study, which they saw as a "further indication of the Jews' faith in the tomorrow and in a Supreme Being."

Consecration (1962 or 63) left to right: Drew Barton, David Sellinger, Barbara Schoenberg, Jill Boniske, Shelley Cohen, Hermene Rocamora, Jeanie Riesenberg, David Friedman, Harriet Patterson, Tracy Kahn, and Gayle Feldman. Rabbi Bloom, Rabbi Unger.

Women in the kitchen! Left to right: Rosalie Schrier, Selma Roth, Janette Kline (behind pole), Evelyn Unger, Pauline Rome, Mildred Michalove, Hilde Hoffman, Evelyn Dave seated in the back, Lorie Shiftan, Elaine Shapiro (next to pole wearing an apron), Rae Garsen (seated in front), ?, ?, and Anne Pearlman, 1952 or 1953. Photo by Geraldine Immel.

3 CONGREGATION BETH ISRAEL

"If you will it, it is no dream." Theodor Hertzl

Asheville was a village before the railroad came in 1880. Then it began to grow quickly, adding immigrants who followed the rail line looking for economic opportunity, patients coming to breathe the clean mountain air, and friends and relatives answering the invitations of those lucky enough to live here.

Bikur Cholim

By 1891 there were enough Jewish residents to form a Conservative synagogue—Congregation Beth HaTephila. Some, however, wanted to follow more familiar, stricter European traditions. By February of 1899 eight men met and officially formed a new Orthodox congregation, naming it Bikur Cholim, "visitation of the sick." In 1904 there was an attempt to consolidate the two synagogues. A meeting to discuss this matter was presided over by Dr. Solomon Schechter, then president of the Jewish Theological Seminary. Asheville, it was felt, did not have a large enough Jewish population to support two synagogues!

September 26, 1916, the day before erev Rosh Hashanah, the synagogue building was finally finished. The total cost had been in excess of $11,000. Suddenly tragedy struck! A fire destroyed the building, leaving only the brick walls standing. The congregation had only insured it for $3,000. The difference was a staggering sum to the small struggling group who had planned and saved for so many years.

Though the synagogue building was small, it had a beautiful interior. Arranged strictly according to Orthodox precepts, the synagogue was visited by many who came just to admire its sanctuary. It was first used for High Holy Day services in 1912, although the building was not fully completed for four more years.

At the 1913 wedding of Ida Pollock and Meyer Levite were many founders of Congregation Bikur Cholim. Rabbi Elias Fox is in the front row wearing a yarmulke. He was the congregation's second rabbi. The older man with the long white beard (next to the groom in the second row) is the father of the groom. He is dressed like a person from "the old country." Lou Pollock, name sake of one of Asheville's Jewish cemeteries, is seventh from the right in the front row. (Additional identifications are available in the digitized Ada and Lou Pollock Collection)

RABBIS

The first religious leader of Bikur Cholim was Rev. Louis Londow, who came from Baltimore in 1897. He also ran a grocery store to supplement his income. In 1948 the congregation purchased a parsonage for their fourteenth rabbi, Rabbi Martin Kessler. Rabbi Kessler was succeeded by Rabbis Alexander Gelberman and Samuel Friedman, who stayed 10 years accepting the challenge of "trying to bring my people back to the old traditional standards of our religion." Since Rabbi Friedman's retirement in 1980, the congregation has seen a succession of spiritual leaders, most notably Rabbis Paul Grob and Shmuel Birnham. Throughout the history of the congregation, there have been many extended periods without a spiritual leader, but knowledgeable lay leaders have again and again stepped in to fill the void.

After using various locations around downtown Asheville, congregants of Bikur Cholim wanted their own synagogue. Land was purchased on South Liberty Street near Woodfin in 1911, where a hotel now stands. Fundraising was a long and arduous process because most members were small business owners or merchants and wealthy members were few.

By 1916 their new sanctuary was finally completed, but it was immediately destroyed by a fire. Fellow Asheville residents came forward with offers of aid, cash donations, building materials and even the services of four Protestant ministers. Plans were immediately begun to rebuild the structure. The Asheville papers periodically reported on the progress of the synagogue's fundraising. Contributors were Jews and gentiles alike, including former Mayor James Eugene Rankin.

Soon after the fire, a group of congregants split off from Bikur Cholim to form a new congregation, Anshei Yeshuran, meaning "Fellowship of the Upright." In the early 1920s that congregation reunited with Bikur Cholim. The synagogue building was finally completed again in 1924 and was the congregation's home for the next 45 years. In 1949 Bikur Cholim affiliated with the United Synagogue of America and became a Conservative congregation. In 1950, Congregation Bikur Cholim changed its name to Congregation Beth Israel.

The Ladies Auxiliary, later known as the Congregation Beth Israel Sisterhood, was started in 1922. Besides fundraising, producing social events and doing beautification projects, they prepared gallons of chicken soup for Jewish patients at local sanitariums who had come to Asheville for a cure for respiratory ailments.

The Men's Club of Bikur Cholim was formed in 1944. Its purpose was to assist the congregation in business and financial affairs and to organize social and recreational events.

Sunday school and the Community Talmud Torah were open to any child regardless of parents' affiliation and were important activities of the congregation.

This chapter is an interpretive panel located at:
229 Murdock Ave, Asheville, NC 28804
Phone: (828) 252-8660
www.bethisraelnc.org

Congregation Beth Israel is especially known for Celebration Israel, an annual festival of Israeli food and culture, which coincides each year with Yom Ha'atzmaut (Israeli Independence Day). 2013 (Courtesy of Patrice Murillo, Wildstarfish Photography)

Congregation Beth Israel

In 1959 in response to rumors that the City of Asheville would be taking their land for a new highway, Congregation Beth Israel purchased the lot it currently occupies. By 1964 the Asheville Development Commission appraised the old building at around $66,000. Later negotiations brought the offer to $88,250 and the City agreed to delay removal of the old South Liberty building until a new one could be completed.

Dr. Dodi Schandler headed the Building Committee and Aaron Schandler the Publicity Committee. Once again a large sum of money needed to be raised. Jerry Sternberg took on that challenge and practically every congregant pitched in to make the new building happen. In 1969, on the day of the last service in the old building, the furnace malfunctioned and filled the structure with smoke. Then President of the congregation, Benson Slosman, said that was is a sign it was time to leave.

During the 1980s women's roles in the synagogue expanded and in 1987 Celine Lurey became the first female president. In 1989 a merger of Congregation Beth HaTephila (which had, by this time, become a Reform Congregation) and Congregation Beth Israel was again debated. By now there was the financial burden of the community supporting three Jewish institutions—the Jewish Community Center being the third. Consensus could not be reached on defining who was a Jew, so the merger again did not succeed.

By the 1990s, Asheville's population began to grow and its Jewish community grew along with it. Congregation Bikur Cholim/Beth Israel has now celebrated its 50th and 100th anniversaries (in 1949 and 1999). Serving the Asheville Jewish Community in three different centuries, it has faced many challenges. Countless numbers of people have given their "time, talent and tzadakah" to insure this congregation continues to offer a variety of religious, educational and cultural programs for adults and children.

4 THE JEWISH COMMUNITY CENTER
The Spirit of Asheville's Jewish Community

By 1916 Asheville had two congregations—Congregation Beth HaTephila and Congregation Bikor Cholim, but one Jewish community. Its youth, including Leo Finkelstein and Julius Levitch, yearned for a meeting place of their own. Rabbi Fox, of Congregation Bikor Cholim (today known as Congregation Beth Israel), who also doubled as a mohel and a schochet, encouraged the boys to be part of a national Jewish movement; so they formed a Young Men's Hebrew Association (YMHA). The organization soon needed more space for more frequent functions, including B'nai B'rith and Hadassah meetings and hospitality to Jewish soldiers serving in World War I. In 1917, the YMHA was reorganized into the Jewish Community Club. The Great Depression of 1929 forced the closure of their own space, but meetings and events continued to be held in rented locations around town—even in the historic S&W cafeteria.

The JCC began to organize in 1938, and officially incorporated in 1940 when the building was acquired. In 1950 the JCC was celebrating its first 10 years of accomplishments: a community-wide Sunday school, organizing dances for soldiers, hosting weddings and offering classes and lectures. Letters of commendation were received from national organizations such as the National Jewish Welfare Board and the B'nai B'rith for achievements of our tiny Jewish community. Slot machines and bingo were big revenue sources. The slot machines were removed in the 1940s before the local authorities could confiscate them!

This chapter is an interpretive panel located at:
236 Charlotte St, Asheville, NC 28801
Phone:(828) 253-0701
www.jcc-asheville.org

Frank Silverman wanted his son to have a place to socialize with other Jewish youth. When Silverman asked others to donate and made a donation himself, Ashevilleans reacted by organizing a Jewish community center. This was in 1938. Once again there would be a location where social, recreational and cultural events could take place. This was during a time of turmoil and heightened anti-Semitism for Jews around the world. Julius Levitch secured a property at 236 Charlotte Street for the community center. With a mortgage of $2,000, the house was remodeled. After WWII began, the Jewish Welfare Board became interested in the JCC. JCC member Sarah Goldstein recalls that the Board funded a weekly Saturday night spaghetti dinner at the JCC for the Jewish soldiers spending the weekend in Asheville from Camp Croft, South Carolina. Several marriages resulted; the first wedding ceremony conducted at the JCC united Ruth and Morris Fox (October 31, 1940).

Going door-to-door, the officers of the nascent community center began to solicit funds. Estelle Marder, who moved to Asheville with her husband and his brother's family in 1939, recalls that three days after they arrived, two men appeared at the door soliciting funds to help buy a building for the Jewish Community Center. "Remember, we're from New York. We didn't know anything called a Jewish Community Center. We knew community centers but we assumed, we didn't even

Hilde Hoffman arrived in Asheville in 1946. She was a Holocaust survivor determined to be involved with her new family- the Asheville Jewish community. She had been a child caregiver as a teenager in Germany so it was natural that she would be a part of the childcare program at the JCC. In appreciation and recognition of her years of service, Hilde's House was named in her honor and continues to serve as the infant daycare. Photo: Top row, left to right: Reed Trotter, Eli Whalen, Hilde Hoffman, Bottom Row: Left to right: "?", Erwin Byrd, Lauren Winner, Anna Stanko.

Kenneth Michalove began the Seven Dwarfs Preschool at the JCC in 1962. It closed for a period and was refounded in 1984 as Shalom Children's Center which continues to receive high ratings for its excellence. "A Special Place for that Special Face: JCC Preschool... because - a good beginning has no end." read a 1979 advertisement. In the 1980s an after school program was developed. High school youth group programs included BBYO and earlier AZT, enabling Jewish youth to connect. Photo: Teva Brown, daughter of former director Geoff Brown.

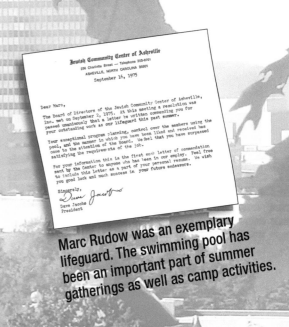

Marc Rudow was an exemplary lifeguard. The swimming pool has been an important part of summer gatherings as well as camp activities.

25

think about it, they were Jewish. Well, we gave them money and they left. And I turned to Dave and I said, 'What's a Jewish Community Center?' He said 'I guess it's for Jews only.' It turned out not to be for Jews only. It's the best thing that happened to us..."

From 1938-1974 Asheville had the only JCC affiliated with the national organization in the state of North Carolina. In 1950 the center had 167 members.

To celebrate Hanukah, a torch run (sometime in the 1980s) began at City Hall, went to Congregation Beth Israel and Congregation Beth HaTephila, ending at the JCC. There, representatives of the Jewish community, as well as other civic and religious leaders, participated in the lighting of the menorah. Throughout its history, the JCC has reached out to the larger Asheville community, strengthening bonds and increasing understanding. From left to right: Marc Rudow, Cindy Corley, Kerry Friedman.

JCC programs are multigenerational. The Maturing Adult Club was formed in the late 1970s and later an elder day care program began at the JCC which was taken over by Jewish Family Services. Left to right: Ilse Hyman, Estelle Marder, Helen Lichenfels Gumpert, unknown, Helen Beninga.

The old house served the community until it was torn down in June 1993 to make way for the current building. Thus began a new opportunity for the JCC to become a cohesive agency ready to take on the challenges of the future - serving not only the Jewish populace, but the greater Asheville community.

5 WE STAND ON THEIR SHOULDERS

Pictured above: Lewis Lipinsky, Coleman Zageir, Samuel Robinson, Morris Karpen, Sprinza Weizenblatt, Ernest Mills and Karl Straus (Courtesy of Ramsey Library Special Collections)

Every community has its visionaries, those special individuals who have clarity of purpose and the spirit of their convictions. The Jewish community, though small, has contributed to the advancement of Asheville well beyond the proportion of its numbers. Many of Asheville's early Jewish residents were business people who were civic minded. They were active in community organizations that included the Masons, Shriners, American Legion, Rotary Club, Lions Clubs International, United Way, Asheville Chamber of Commerce, Knights of Pythias, Benevolent & Protective Order of Elks and Kiwanis. They took the Hebrew phrase *tikkun olam,* which means "repairing or healing the world," as their responsibility to improve Asheville and were acknowledged by the greater community for their deeds. Today we can still see the results of their efforts. Here we acknowledge only a few of the many Jews who affected the larger Asheville community in so many ways.

Jewish Support for Mission Saint Joseph Hospital

Jewish donors and volunteers have contributed to Mission and St. Joseph Hospitals (now merged together as Mission-St. Joseph's Health System) for many years. Shirley and Harry Blomberg are noted among the significant donors to the hospital, as are Marilyn and Buddy Patton and Audrey and Robert Bayer. Many women, including Marilyn Patton, Dorothy Fliegel, Joan Rocamora and Arlene Doloboff spent thousands of hours volunteering at various activities including the gift shop. Marilyn Patton once remarked that she had done everything but surgery during her years of service to the hospital. Arlene Doloboff has logged over 15,000 hours in St. Joseph hospital's gift shop.

Jewish Support for the University of North Carolina Asheville

The University of North Carolina took over Asheville Buncombe College and built the present-day UNC Asheville campus in 1969. Buildings there display the names of honored long-time supporters such as Lewis Lipinsky, Coleman Zageir, Samuel Robinson, Morris Karpen, Sprinza Weizenblatt and Ernest Mills, along with a sports track named for Karl Straus. Most of these individuals contributed not only funds, but also time and effort, helping the University to grow into the success it is today.

The following biographical panels can be found on the campus of UNC Asheville in the buildings that honor the legacies of their namesakes. The Karl Straus panel will be placed by the track that honors him.

The Ronald Manheimer panel was a later addition placed to honor Ron for his service as director of the North Carolina Center for Creative Retirement, today named the Osher Life Long Learning Institute (OLLI). It can be found in the Reuter Center, Manheimer room.

SOLOMON LIPINSKY
Bon Marché

Solomon Lipinsky is first listed in the Asheville census in 1880, twenty-four years old and living with his wife and brother-in-law in a boarding house on Woodfin Street. Early on, he worked as a clerk at S. Whitlock & Company on South Main near Eagle Street. By 1887 he owned his own store at 46 South Main

Solomon Lipinsky (1856–1925) was a retail visionary who brought to Asheville the new ideas used in big city department stores, the modern way to shop in the Gilded Age of the late 1800s.

A leader in Asheville's early civic life, Lipinsky was a charter member of Temple Beth HaTephila, a leader of the Royal Arcanum and many other fraternal orders and a highly regarded citizen.

Street (now Biltmore Avenue). In 1890, he and his half-sister had a store together, Lipinsky & Ellick, at 30 South Main. They called it Bon Marché.

Bon Marché was an Asheville landmark for 90 years. Its success followed the growth of Asheville. In 1889 Asheville was a small mountain town with dirt streets, home to 10,000 people. By 1925 the population had nearly tripled. The streets were paved and lined with stores. Bon Marché, one of the state's largest department stores at that time, was considered by many to be one of its finest. Family owned and operated, three generations of Lipinskys ran Bon Marché.

Louis Lipinsky, Sr., Solomon's youngest son, (1888–1966) married Clara Nathan of Charlotte, NC, in 1919. He worked in Bon Marché for 28 years, managing the Charlotte store and then the Asheville store. His father's legacy of civic participation continued in the younger Lipinsky who worked tirelessly to build a better campus for Asheville-Biltmore College. He led an effort to persuade the University of North Carolina to make Asheville-Biltmore a part of the UNC system, which it did in 1969.

Lipinsky Auditorium at UNC Asheville is named in his honor.

March 3, 1938

Dear Louis:

...I am certainly interested in your project, because although I did not know your father except by sight, I have known all you boys all my life, and Bon Marché is such a landmark in Asheville life that if I ever heard anything had happened to it I think I should feel almost as if Beaucatcher Mountain had been violently removed from the local landscape by some force of nature. I know that as long as I can remember, at any rate, it has always stood with the women folk at home for the best in merchandise and fashion.

...it may interest and amuse you to know that when I first saw Paris, as a kid of twenty-four, I could not quite get used to the fact that they had a Bon Marché, as well; I kept wondering what the hell they were doing with our name.

...Sincerely yours, Tom Wolfe

Thomas Wolfe wrote to Louis Lipinsky in preparation for the 50th anniversary of Bon Marché in 1939: (Courtesy of Carl Van Vechten - Van Vechten Collection at Library of Congress)

Go West With Success

The merchants had a saying, "Go west with success." That is exactly what Bon Marché did after a series of locations on South Main Street, now Biltmore Avenue. In 1911, it moved to Patton Avenue. From there it moved further west to Haywood Street where it remained, in two different locations, for 55 years.

BEFORE 1911

One of Bon Marché's several early South Main Street Locations (now Biltmore Avenue)

The beginnings of Bon Marché's reign as western North Carolina's longest-lived premier shopping emporium came with the store's move to Patton Avenue.

1911–1923

Northwest corner of Patton and Lexington Avenues. The old Berkeley Hotel on the corner of Patton Avenue and Lexington Avenue the current location of the Kress Building.

This new store featured elaborate displays in its windows, clearly marked prices on each item, merchandise separated by department and Asheville's first public elevator, a novelty and attraction for many.

1923–1936

Corner of Haywood Street and Battery Park Avenue

Bon Marché moved to a much larger building constructed by E.W. Grove in 1923 for his friend Solomon Lipinsky. It was built to Lipinsky's specifications using the best fireproof construction materials of the time. Ivey's Department Store moved into this building in 1937 and it now houses the Haywood Park Hotel.

1937–1979

33 HAYWOOD STREET

This is the store most people remember as Bon Marché. It was at this location for 42 years. During that time, the store sponsored daily radio broadcasts, brought in famous designers and make-up artists and was an official sales agent for Girl Scout and Boy Scout uniforms. The business was sold to the Automatic Service Company of Atlanta in 1969. This location closed in July of 1979, when malls and strip shopping centers became popular and downtown began a period of decline. This building is currently occupied by Earth Guild.

 Photographs courtesy Pack Library, North Carolina desk, Joanne Lipinsky Edwinn, Ball Collection, UNC Asheville Ramsey Library Special Collections

COLEMAN ZAGEIR
An Unsung Hero

Every town has its legendary businesses and The Man Store was certainly one of those. Most people who lived in or anywhere near Asheville from 1922 until the store left downtown in the early 1970s were familiar with it. Coleman Zageir (1894-1975) opened The Man Store in 1922 and operated it for more than forty years at the same location, 22 Patton Avenue. The Man Store was sold to Hart, Schaffner & Marx in 1963. It eventually moved to the Asheville Mall, underwent a name change and closed.

"The stories about him are many: For years he gave members of the graduating class of Asheville High School (he was a member of the Class of 1912) maroon and black ties [the school colors]. Then there were the [anonymous] scholarships he awarded needy seniors giving them a chance at college… Then there were the depression years when, with banks failing, monthly statements from the store were never mailed."

— Asheville Times, "UNC-A Building To Be Named for Civic Leader Coleman Zageir" May, 1974

Zageir Dies Here; Civic Leader

31

He was a modest man, stating, "If you are a member of the community, that's a responsibility you should recognize and assume." Yet he disliked publicity and only gave three interviews to the media in his lifetime. His service was recognized by the University of North Carolina at Asheville when one of its new classroom buildings was named the Coleman Zageir Social Sciences Building in 1974.

1930s

Interior of The Man Store. Coleman Zageir on right next to tie rack.

Zageir was, like many of Asheville's Jewish merchants, active in the local civic community. He served on the board of directors of the Asheville Area Chamber of Commerce, the Asheville Merchants Association and the United Way.

An Unsung Hero…

"Coleman always chewed a cigar. He never lit it – he chewed it all the time. Kind of an odd thing… He just had a way of making people feel special.

And my daddy didn't have any money… He owned a funeral home in Bryson City. So we'd go over [to Asheville] and he would refinance a vehicle at Wachovia [Bank]… and then he would go down and pay Coleman Zageir for what he bought the year before, and then he would buy whole new outfits for the coming year…

He was always one year behind with Coleman. But [Coleman] didn't care, because he knew daddy was good for it and was always going to show up around Christmas time. Kind of a neat thing."

— **Reg Moody**
Owner, Moody's Funeral Home, Sylva, NC

"I loved that man. I got my first suit there when I was twelve. He threw in a shirt and a tie for free. He had me for life."

— **Chan Gordon**
Owner, The Captain's Bookshelf, Asheville

"I had graduated from high school and was accepted at Asheville-Biltmore College [now UNC-A] and I did not own a suit. I wanted one for college. So I went to The Man Store to buy one. I had on a beautiful tan summer suit and the tailor was marking the pants length while I stood in front of the three-way mirror. And Mr. Zageir walked by. And he stopped and he looked at me in that suit. He said something to the salesman, who answered him back.

"And he came over and said to me, 'One shoulder is higher than the other. We need to cut the padding down.' And he took that chalk from the tailor and he marked up the shoulder with it. He was walking all around me marking up that suit. His

LATE 1960s

The Man Store, corner of Lexington and Patton Avenue.

Other family members also had stores in downtown. His older brother, Robert, owned a men's clothing store at 8 South Main (now Biltmore Avenue) from 1900-1929 and their relative, Maer Zageir, was proprietor of clothing stores at different downtown locations from 1904 until the early 1930s. Mrs. Lena Zageir is listed in the Asheville City Directory as owner of a clothing store at 44 Biltmore Avenue in 1915.

hands were just flying with that chalk. It was a twenty-six dollar suit. He had hundred dollar suits in his store. But he was treating me like I was one of his best customers. And when I got that suit, it looked wonderful on. I had it for years.

"And I know why he did it—he wanted me to buy all my suits there. The salesman told him it was my first suit and he wanted it to fit me like a custom-tailored suit. He treated me like a millionaire and I know a lot of other men had the exact same experience. I always bought my suits at The Man Store."

— Joe Bly
U.S. Post Office, retired.
Host, Shindig on the Green, retired, Asheville

"One of Asheville's now prominent doctors came out of the service following World War II hoping to set up practice. *It would be a costly venture for this young physician who had little more than the uniform he came home with… The young doctor dropped in and told Coleman his problem. He didn't have a practice, but was determined to establish one. Mr Zageir quietly smiled and proceeded to outfit the young doctor. No bill was ever mailed. A simple oral statement as the doctor left: 'When you can.' Four years later the debt was paid. There were many others who received similar help in launching their careers."*

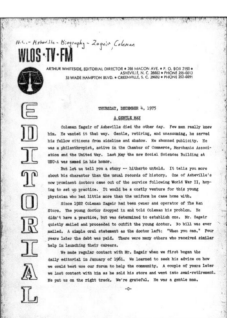

—Arthur Whiteside, Editorial Director, WLOS-TV
Delivered as tribute upon death of Coleman Zageir daily editorial for Dec. 4, 1975

SAMUEL ROBINSON
Man of Passion and Principle

Samuel Robinson was a man of action and deep principle, a leader by example. He came from Russia to the United States during a wave of Eastern European immigration, arriving in Galveston, Texas in 1901. At the University of Texas, he earned a degree in engineering, then worked in Texas fisheries, Louisiana oil fields, and as a surveyor for Houston harbor. His 1913 college yearbook described him as having an "inborn desire to eradicate aristocratic tendencies." It continued, "Sam will have an idea on any subject, no matter how insignificant."

Dr. Samuel Robinson hiking in the mountains he loved (1937). The environment was one of his passions. An avid hiker, he kept a detailed record of every hike he made. An active member of the Carolina Mountain Club until he deemed their hikes too easy, Dr. Robinson founded a hiking group (he called) the Wilderness Hikers. He volunteered with the American Forestry Association and campaigned at length, with others, to name a 6,000-foot peak in the Great Smoky Mountains "Masa Knob" in honor of George Masa, a Japanese immigrant and founding member of the Carolina Mountain Club who devoted much of his life to photographing and mapping the Smokey Mountain National Park and the Appalachian Trail.

Whiteside Mountain hike June 2, 1940, Leah Robinson Karpen and Michael Robinson.

As engineering was not his life's calling, he proceeded to obtain a degree in optometry. His father Daniel operated a jewelry store in downtown Asheville between 1915 and 1942. He told his son he believed there would be opportunity for him here in western North Carolina. The young Dr. Robinson then moved to Asheville to begin a practice in optometry. Thriving in this new mountain environment, Dr. Robinson immersed himself in numerous civic duties, including serving on the [Asheville] Metropolitan Planning Board. His many accomplishments resulted in the naming of Robinson Hall on the campus of the University of North Carolina-Asheville in his memory.

Whiteside Mountain

Sunday June 2, 1940. It is a warm, partly cloudy day. We leave Asheville at 8:45. We cross through Cashiers then re-ascend the Blue Ridge. On foot we follow the old road and then worn trail towards top...The views are spectacular to the southeast is the famous preicipice said to be the highest in Eastern America. There are patches of vegetation at upper rim of mountain hundreds of feet of bare...rock below this rim.

We walk along crest of mountain to its northern extremity, then return to lunch at the top. After a long rest we retrace our steps down from the mountain...Arrive Asheville at 6:45.

Excerpt from Mountain Memories, Volume III A Record of My Mountaineering, Hiking Trips Outings, & Travels, Dr. S. Robinson, Asheville, N.C. pages 51-52. (Unpublished.)

Dr. Samuel Robinson in front of his optometry office at 78 Patton Avenue, in downtown Asheville (1936). During the over 55 years he practiced optometry, he performed his own lab work, wrote and presented several papers that addressed difficult optometric problems, and created his own method of glaucoma therapy. A strong proponent of equal rights, Dr. Robinson never turned any patients away because of their race or inability to pay, and he instituted a first-come first-serve policy despite the segregation protocols of his day. He believed in treating his patients equally, regardless of social status or ethnicity.

Samuel and Esther Robinson in 1972. They met in Asheville where her mother Jennie Kroman owned a women's hat shop, Paris Millinery, sharing a partition wall with Robinson's optometry practice at 78 Patton Avenue. Esther later managed his office and was a great supporter of Samuel's causes. She jokingly referred to herself as a "hiking widow" on weekends.

As a proponent of civil rights, Samuel strove to integrate the Boy Scouts of America, an organization in which he was active for more than 25 years on the local, as well as the national level. The photograph at left shows him receiving the Silver Beaver award for his work in scouting.

Dr. Samuel Robinson 1891-1973

MORRIS KARPEN
A Man with Vision and Ideas

Morris Karpen (1916-2002) was a modest man who never sought recognition for his accomplishments or his generosity. Respectful of each and every person, he touched the lives of many. He is remembered for his energy and initiative as well as being a mentor and caring benefactor. "The generosity with which Morris lived his life was and forever will be an inspiration to us all." *UNCA Chancellor James Mullen.*

Morris Karpen pictured here in 1929, at the age of thirteen, as a Bar Mitzvah (Jewish rite of passage into adulthood). This religious training influenced his philosophy of life. Morris always stood up for people who were not able to represent themselves and he pursued social issues even if they were not popular. He believed that communication and coordination were a much better use of energy than conflict. "He was a kind and gentle individual who made us feel better about being members of the human community" said Warrene Williams in a tribute to Morris.

The original sign from Karpen Steel in Farmingdale, New York. Willing to take risks, with little money, and lots of hope, perseverance and know-how, Morris founded the company in 1950. He had an incredible intellect and could take an idea and turn it into something that would have meaning. In his 70's he was still thinking of new ideas.

The Karpens were a working class family who lived in New York City. After completing high school, Morris attended Mechanics Institute, a tuition-free technical school for people working in the building trades. There he learned drafting and three-dimensional thinking, skills which were

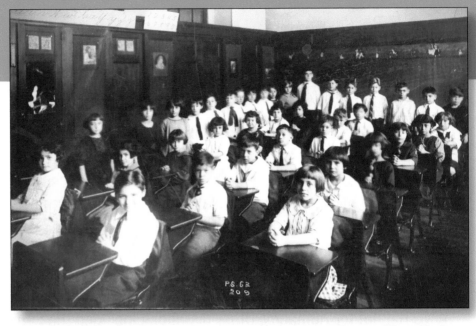

the foundation of his career. The picture above is New York City Public School 62, Bronx, New York. Morris is the 4th from the left in the last row.

Morris was a hands-on type of leader. He designed and built several Karpen Steel facilities and some of the equipment, as well as several family homes. He always treated his employees as family, he the father figure one would not hesitate to go to for advice or learning. Morris instituted family- and female-supportive programs long before they were in vogue. He cared for his employees and offered many opportunities for them to do well and make a good living. By promoting labor practices not common in a craft industry, he insured that he always had qualified workers. His philosophy was that one should hire the best people you can find and let them do their jobs. "They might not do things exactly the way you would, but you might be surprised to see that their ways are actually better than your way," he once said. In addition to his mechanical abilities, Morris was a successful vegetable gardener. The picture above was taken at the Karpen Steel factory, Morris is on the very left.

Need a door in a hurry?

When you have an urgent request, Karpen delivers! Our custom shop fabricates hollow metal doors and frames to any dimension— shipped in 10 working days from receipt of your order. We can supply UL labeled doors and frames when needed. Write or call today for our catalog. We won't leave you backed up against the wall.

Karpen STEEL PRODUCTS

Karpen Steel Products became successful by filling a niche. They manufactured fire-rated doors and frames in custom sizes and shapes and promised 10-day delivery, which transformed the hollow metal industry.

Helping The Community

The Karpens spent more than 25 years donating their time, energy and money to a variety of causes and organizations. "We tried to help in the community where we saw need," Leah said. Their generosity launched nonprofit groups and endowed Karpen and Robinson Halls at UNC Asheville. At Warren Wilson College their donations brought students to Western North Carolina from around the world and built Morris' pavilion. They have also given seed grants for Helpmate battered women's shelter, Hospitality House transitional faculties for homeless men and women,Self-help Credit Union's western office and its Working Women's Loan Fund and WNC Habitat for Humanity. Other donations included the Laurel Forum in Karpen Hall, the YWCA, Manna Food Bank, Asheville Art Museum, Buncombe County Literacy Council and Congregation Beth HaTephila.

Positive thinking and hard work! When Morris retired, he and his wife, Leah, moved back to her home town, Asheville. Morris was a workaholic and retirement was not for him. He soon started two businesses in Weaverville: a new Karpen Steel factory and Laser Precision Cutting. The latter company offers a faster, more economical method to produce parts for sheet metal and machine shops by cutting the metal with a laser instead of using traditional machining methods. Being in retirement businesses, Morris was able to focus on sharing his knowledge with younger workers. After a trip to China, Morris explained this philosophy: "I want to use the brain of older people to teach the young."

Leah and Morris Karpen in 1987. Wed in 1944 while Morris was serving in the army in World War II, they were devoted to each other. When Leah brought Morris to meet her family, her father, Dr. Samuel Robinson (Robinson Hall) took Morris on a hike, 5 miles straight up a mountain and 5 miles back down. Morris felt this was a test, which he later said he must have passed, as he was accepted into the family.

In 1994 the Karpens learned of the scarcity of soccer fields. This prompted Morris to make one of his most visible and valuable contributions. He donated the property next to Karpen Steel for use as youth soccer fields. This gift has helped thousands of children learn skills they might otherwise not have had the opportunity to learn and was the donation which made Morris the proudest. "Seeing the children playing there was all I needed.' he said.

Photographs Courtesy of the UNC Asheville Ramsey Library Special Collections

SPRINZA WEIZENBLATT
Hope and Perseverance Bring a Brighter Future

In the late 1920s, Asheville ophthalmologist Harry Briggs went to Austria to study at the world famous Vienna Eye Clinic. While there, he met Sprinza Weizenblatt, a brilliant young doctor who spoke fluent English. She so impressed Dr. Briggs that he invited her to move to Asheville to be his associate, a position which paid $100 a month. Arriving in 1928, Weizenblatt and Briggs practiced together several years, but Sprinza soon built her own large practice specializing in the treatment of eye diseases.

Dr. Weizenblatt

Sprinza developed an outstanding reputation among her patients for treating equally everyone who sought her service, black or white, rich or poor. Using a generous portion of her income, she maintained a cash box in the waiting room. If she thought a patient could not pay for a treatment, the receptionist was instructed to take the required cash from the box and to tell the patient an unnamed benefactor had donated the money. She always made time for her patients, during all hours of the day or night. Patients knew they could count on her.

Sprinza Weizenblatt (1895 - 1987) was born in what is now Romania in the province of Bukovina in the foothills of the Carpathian Mountains. She and her family fled to Vienna, Austria before World War I in order to escape persecution.

Philanthropy

Never forgetting her struggle for an education, Sprinza donated sizeable sums of money to educational institutions including UNC Asheville, Brandeis University, Weizmann Institute of Science in Israel and Montreat, Warren Wilson and Mars Hill Colleges. Her medical contributions include the establishment of the Memorial Mission Eye Service at Mission Hospital and a well-baby clinic on the Cherokee Indian reservation.

Sprinza raised prize-winning orchids, which she said reminded her of birds' eyes. She knew the Latin names of many flowers and had a love of nature, which she attributed to her father.

Learning

Sprinza had no time for idle chit chat, she told her neighbors. Throughout her career, she found time to conduct medical research, publishing her findings and presenting them at national and international conferences. Her voracious appetite for culture often took her on trips to New York City to see operas, plays and concerts, while leaving time to evaluate the newest instruments for eye surgery. "New York City was the closest thing to cosmopolitan Vienna she could get," remembers her friend Dr. Margaret Burns. Her thirst for intellectual entertainment also drew her to people and events at Black Mountain College (see photo). She was determined to learn something new every day.

Black Mountain College 1933-1957, a progressive college for the arts in the Asheville area. Sprinza would attend performances there and knew many of the faculty. She found her cultural peer group in the artists, writers and musicians who came here. Many had fled oppression in Germany when Hitler closed the Bauhaus. Hertha Horwitz, Sprinza's niece, remembers that Joseph Albers, head of the Painting Department who later went on to head the Yale University Department of Design, offered Sprinza a painting. She turned it down because she didn't like the colors. However, Albers' wife, Annie, an accomplished fabric artist, designed the fabric for Sprinza's home drapery and furniture.

Sprinza at the Audubon Camp, Hog Island, Maine, 1951. Sprinza, just 4 feet 11 inches, was true to her name, Esperanza, from the Latin meaning "hope." She was direct, Germanic and professional with her patients, with a decided impish side. Dr. Anne Sagberg, an Asheville psychiatrist, remembered the first time she saw Sprinza, in 1956, at the age of 60: she was walking around a swimming pool on her hands. Sprinza took up surfing at the age of 70, and backpacked through Alaska carrying a 50-pound knapsack and pitching her own tent while in her 80s. She sent her great-niece a postcard saying that Alaska was wonderful, but she was having a little difficulty with the tent!

Health

Her interest in fitness and good health served her well. She advised people in her instructive tone not to eat white bread and chocolate and told her great-niece to eat eggs if she wanted to grow. Ironically, Sprinza lost her sight for the last five years of her life. She died at the age of 92.

Sprinza Weizenblatt is remembered not just for her treatment of patients and her charitable contributions, but also for her zest for life and constant thirst for knowledge.

Vienna Eye Clinic (1926 or 1927). During a tumultuous political time in Austria this indigent Jewish woman overcame the odds against her success and was able to study through merit scholarships and a focused determination. Ranked first in her class, she was glad to wear her white medical coat to hide her worn clothing underneath. (Sprinza is in the center of the photo in the second row 7th from the left.)

Asheville's women physicians periodically had lunch together. The photograph above is a welcome lunch for Dr. Patricia Dodd who had just opened a surgical practice here (1957). Sprinza brought her a corsage made from an orchid grown in her greenhouse. When Dr. Dodd asked Sprinza how women doctors are treated here. Sprinza replied, "They are tolerated."

Seated from left to right: Charmen Carroll (psychiatrist), Irma Henderson, Louise Galloway. Standing: Margery Lord (second from left), Polly Shuford (third from left), Pat Dodd (fourth from left), Sprinza Weizenblatt (fifth from left), (unknown)

As intense about her hobbies as she was about her patients, Sprinza was an outdoor enthusiast who enjoyed backpacking in the Smoky Mountains and was an active member of the Carolina Mountain Hiking Club, the oldest hiking and trail maintaining club in Western North Carolina. (Sprinza is in the checked shirt in the front row on the left.)

Sprinza loved to travel and went all over the world, including Nepal, Russia, China where she observed acupuncture, Morocco, Kyoto Japan and Southern Africa with a group of physicians to care for people suffering from eye diseases. (Pictured above on the left she is on a trip to Mexico with Clementine Douglas, a weaver and owner of the Spinning Wheel craft shop.)

Photographs Courtesy of the UNC Asheville Ramsey Library Special Collections, the estate of Hazel Larsen Archer, the Black Mountain College Seal 1934-1935 designed by Josef Albers, the Black Mountain College Museum + Arts Center

ERNEST A. MILLS
Gave Back to His Community

Ernest A. Mills (1908-1989) was a hands-on manager, involved in every aspect of his manufacturing business. He also had a passion for the theater and was a close friend of American playwright and screenwriter, Clifford Odets.

Ernest A. Mills (Ernie) rose from humble beginnings to become a successful businessman, civic leader and philanthropist who gave back to the Asheville Community. His daughter, Pamela Mills Turner, described him as "firm, but fair, with a generous heart."

Ernie grew up in New York City and was drawn to the excitement of Wall Street where he began his career as a messenger. Determined to create an impact he, advanced quickly and soon became a trader on the stock market. Ernie would later tell his friend and Asheville icon, Karl Straus, that working on Wall Street during the crash in 1929 is where he would acquire a more measured view of the world of business.

Albina Mills (1914-1994) was always generous with her volunteer time. As a registered nurse, she participated in Red Cross Blood drives and served on the board of the Orthopedic Hospital (now Care Partners). She also supported the Asheville Community Theater (ACT).

In 1935, during the Great Depression, Ernie founded Mills Strap and Novelty, a notions and undergarment manufacturing business, where he worked with his father Victor, and his brothers, Larry and Harry. In 1942, during World War II, the US government sought factories with experience in sewing nylon to manufacture parachutes. Mills quickly transformed its operation to support the US military, a decision that would impact not only the future of the company, but also Ernie's family.

When the Korean War broke out, Mills needed to expand their parachute operation because of growing demand.

They looked to the South where a strong textile industry flourished. The location for the new plant was narrowed down to Durham and Asheville. On the day of Mill's visit, Durham was experiencing a heat wave, and Asheville was cool and crisp. Knowing he would live where he worked, Asheville was the natural choice. Asheville was chosen for its quality of life, strong sense of community and skilled workforce. In return, the region gained a man who was committed to the economic development, cultural growth and the strengthening of educational resources in Western North Carolina.

Mills' generosity was often anonymous; and in addition to supporting major charities he

Ernie receiving an honorary Doctorate of Laws degree from UNC Asheville Chancellor David Brown (1988). "As one whose faithful leadership and service sustained and nurtured the development of the University as it grew..." (Excerpt from the resolution of the UNC Asheville Board of Trustees, May 7, 1988)

supported many of his employees and others during times of crisis. In fact, one winter Mills stepped in to pay the heating bills of a local college as it struggled to pay its bills. He did this without recognition or request for repayment.

Ernie Mills was an intelligent, intense man who used his talents and energy to lead a useful and purposeful life. He was always generous with his time and money, especially

Ernie working at the Mills Strap and Novelty Company in New York City in the 1930's. They manufactured undergarments and novelty accessories.

where education was concerned. He provided scholarship funding to the University of North Carolina-Asheville. His philanthropy, which helped guide the growth and prosperity of the

Jim Turner (son-in-law), Albina Mills (wife), Ernest Mills, and Pam Turner (daughter and former member of the UNC Asheville Board of Trustees)

community, included serving as a trustee or board member of several organizations: Asheville-Buncombe Technical Community College, St. Joseph's Hospital and UNC Asheville. Because of the lack of educational opportunities during his youth, one of Ernest Mills' goals was to provide men and women greater access to higher education. Ernest Mills' substantial contributions are still recognized and honored by UNC Asheville today, where Mills Hall stands in grateful tribute.

Not much has changed in the hands-on manufacture of parachutes since the 1950's when this photo was taken of an assembly worker. Quality control is taken very seriously as there is no room for error. The factory continues its operations today supplying a variety of parachutes to the United States government and internationally.

The parachute business flourished; and in 1959, Mills Manufacturing moved from rented space to their own facility. They hired a food service managed by the local Lions Club and staffed by visually impaired workers. Their factory was one of the first new Asheville plants to have integrated bathrooms. (l-r Roy Sanders, Larry Mills, John Knox, Larry Windman, Dick Lamb, Hoonard Spahn, John Scheer, Ernie Mills)

KARL STRAUS
Community Leader Who Fought Intolerance

Giving Back to the Community

Because Karl felt his community had offered him extraordinary opportunities and deserved his everlasting thanks, he wanted to make a difference in Asheville's civic, educational, philanthropic and religious endeavors, always in an effort to "give back." He served on numerous boards, including: UNC Asheville Board of Trustees and its Foundation Board, Memorial Mission Hospital, Wachovia Bank, Congregation Beth HaTephila and the Community Foundation of Western North Carolina. He considered intolerance, prejudice and discrimination a disease to be eliminated, and so volunteered his time with the Asheville Chapter of the National Association of Christians and Jews and the Asheville Buncombe Human Relations Council.

Karl Straus (b. 1921) practiced law in Asheville for over 50 years.

Coming to America

Harry Straus brought his nephew Karl to New York City in 1936 from Mannheim, Germany, to remove him from the danger of the Nazis. After high school and secretarial school, Karl came to Pisgah Forest to work at his Uncle Harry's cigarette paper manufacturing plant, Ecusta Paper Company. In 1942, Karl tried to join the military, but was rejected as an "enemy alien." As soon as he became an American citizen, he became a member of the US Army Air Corps, then transferred to the Allied Military Government for postwar Germany.

He was assigned to the US Treasury Department as a civilian officer, where he served in the Financial Intelligence Division. Karl received a bronze star for his work in the denazification program of the Allied Military Government.

Karl took the North Carolina Bar Exam in 1953 and partnered with his father-in-law, Joseph A. Patla, to form Patla & Straus, which today is the firm Patla, Straus, Robinson and Moore. Karl is in the sixth row, fourth from the right In front of the Buncombe County Courthouse.

After World War II

Returning to the United States in 1946, Karl benefited from the GI Bill to attend college and law school at New York University, while also working at a gas station. He chose this path over the objections of his Uncle Harry, who did not think Karl needed a law degree to return to work at Ecusta! Karl did return to western North Carolina and settled in Asheville after a short stint practicing law in New York. It was here in Asheville, that Karl practiced law.

The Ecusta Paper Corporation, Pisgah Forest, was started by Harry Straus, uncle of Karl. Plant construction was completed in 1939. Its location near Brevard provided clean water and the workforce necessary to supply the U.S. tobacco industry with American manufactured cigarette papers made with flax. Prior to this time, all cigarette papers were imported from France and were made using rags. With World War II about to begin, RJ Reynolds and others realized that they could not rely on suppliers in Europe and that the war would increase demand for cigarettes.

Karl understood that leading others to give has the greatest impact as a philanthropist. He demonstrated dedicated service to the University of North Carolina at Asheville while serving as chair of the Board of Trustees and later chair of the university Foundation Board. For his service and support to the university, UNC Asheville awarded Karl the chancellor's medallion in 1989 and also named its track in his honor in 1992. In this 1989 photo, Karl is recognized for his board service by Chancellor David G. Brown.

Karl went to college on an urban campus. He dreamed of what it would have been like to attend a school like the University of North Carolina-Asheville in such a beautiful location. Always athletic, Karl would come to campus to play tennis. On one of these visits, he met Chancellor William E. Highsmith who suggested he become involved with his adopted campus and he did! Karl Straus and Chancellor Samuel Schuman at the dedication of Straus Track, October 1992, are pictured above.

While working at a New York law firm Karl reacquainted himself with Sylvia Patla, whom he had met 13 years earlier at Ecusta in Pisgah Forest. Sylvia had come to New York to experience life outside of her native Asheville. When Karl was offered a job in Waynesville for the astronomical sum of $6,000 annually, they both quit their jobs and moved back. Sylvia Patla Straus (1922-2013) and Karl Straus are pictured above. (Courtesy of Sylvia Straus)

"...This occasion is of particular significance to me as it was twenty-seven years ago almost to the day that I stood in this very courtroom where you are standing now and received my certificate of naturalization—when I became an American citizen just like you have become American citizens this morning.

"This occasion very beautifully dramatizes and gives living proof of the opportunities of this land of ours and it is my honor today, as president of the Buncombe County Bar Association, to give to each of you a pamphlet in which are contained the principles of right and justice.

"The pamphlet, entitled 'Charters of Freedom: The Declaration of Independence, the Constitution and the Bill of Rights'... embodies in its structure an accumulation of the wisdom and the genius of generations of men and women. We as individual citizens seem unimportant and small. Yet it is the individual...that justifies the existence of our state, and the system of our government—and we give the government the responsibility to maintain the conditions, the peace, the order and the justice, under which we, the individuals, can strive and under which we, the individuals, are given an opportunity to develop to the fullest all the abilities with which God has endowed us.

It is very appropriate therefore that on this occasion you are presented with copies of these documents, for this charter of freedom has formed the basis and given the inspiration for so many of the changes our country has directly and indirectly brought about in the thoughts and philosophies and in the betterment of peoples all over the world—and it is the same charter of freedom which has been the fundamental basis for so many of the all-important changes that have been brought about in our country in the past decades.

So, on this day of your naturalization, I hope and trust that in return for the right and privilege of citizenship, you will assume one of the responsibilities of citizenship, the active participation in all the affairs of our government... It is my firm conviction that if as a nation and as a people we are to grow and prosper and achieve all that which we are capable of achieving, it can only be within the fundamental principles of these documents, our charter of freedom."

RONALD MANHEIMER
Redefining the Meaning of Retirement

Ronald J. Manheimer has spent his career guiding recent retirees on new paths of learning, relationships and involvement. He has enabled them to feel empowered to pursue unfulfilled hopes and expectations.

More than a PhD-trained philosopher and teacher, Ron had practical experience as a leader of lifelong learning opportunities and a life transition facilitator. Early in his career he discovered that when job opportunities arose and he was asked to start a new program, he always said, "Yes!"– launching into the unknown rather than the known path. His success came from taking the approach: Go learn about it and go do it!

Coming to UNC Asheville

Ron served in various posts in California and Washington State and as Director of older adult education at The National Council on Aging in Washington, DC. In 1988, Ron received an offer he could not refuse. UNC Asheville's then chancellor David Brown wanted to develop a national model for creative retirement. Chancellor Brown had gone so far as to write a lengthy brochure detailing a wide array of program offerings – dreaming big about this brand

Creative retirement is a notion found in cultures around the world. In many other countries, leaders have realized that their large populations of healthy older adults want to continue to be a vital part of society, and want to continue to learn. Ron Manheimer, Robert (Bob) Davis, and Denise Snodgrass traveled by invitation to Taiwan to present NCCCR's model for older adult programing at an international conference in 2008. Bob was then chair of the NCCCR's Steering Council, while Denise was assistant director of the center.

new endeavor. Handing the brochure to Ron, Chancellor Brown simply said, "Let's try them all and see which ones work!" That set the tone for this ambitious and innovative program, and Ron became the first director of the North Carolina Center for Creative Retirement (NCCCR). The NCCCR was renamed the Osher Lifelong Learning Institute (OLLI) at UNC Asheville in 2012.

NCCCR flourished, incorporating Ron's philosophy on creative retirement and capturing his vision. By 1998, a space shortage led to the idea of building a structure solely to house NCCCR. With help from UNC Asheville's Board of Trustees, who provided 5.5 acres of campus land, and UNC Asheville's Development Office, a team of volunteers and NCCCR staff raised $4.5 million for construction of a 20,000 square foot building. Named the Reuter Center, it opened in June of 2003. Ron had the vision and worked with others to make it a reality, never dreaming they could raise so much from individual contributions.

Today, Ron feels that the challenge at OLLI will be to serve an even larger number of constituents with diverse

In graduate school Ron studied philosophy and human development, receiving a PhD from the Board of Studies in History of Consciousness, University of California, Santa Cruz, in 1973. While there he was fortunate to have future colleague Harry "Rick" Moody as his roommate. Says Ron, "Some of us have 'messengers' in our lives, people who bring ideas and opportunities to our attention, often unbidden ones. Rick has been one of those people for me. He was the one who suggested that I might enjoy teaching older adults which led to my first volunteer gig in Olympia, Washington; and he recommended me for a job at The National Council on Aging as director of older adult education (for which I was hired)." Rick served for a short time on NCCCR's National Advisory Board, which existed from 1989 to about 1995.

The Gurus of Creative Aging, Rick Moody (left) and Ron are pictured in front of Windsor Castle in England in 2012 near where they were attending a symposium on aging and spirituality.

Thanks to innovators like Ron, we can now say we live in the era of creative aging. At OLLI, newcomers find groups of learners contributing to the larger Asheville area community. The organization thrived under Ron's leadership, with adventurous programs like the College for Seniors, Leadership Asheville Seniors, and the Senior Academy for Intergenerational Learning. Some retirees moved to Asheville after experiencing one of the annual Creative Retirement Exploration Weekends. Pictured are Ron Manheimer and Denise Snodgrass at a 1950s theme party at the Reuter Center in 2008.

interests and learning styles. These participants have one thing in common: they see aging not as a time to avoid risk, but as a period of vibrancy and dreams realized.

Early Life

Born in 1943 and raised in Detroit, Ron graduated from Monteith College, an innovative, liberal arts college within Wayne State University. There he discovered people had the capacity to be their own teachers and to teach others. Ron traveled to Israel in the summer of 1966 and worked on a kibbutz. Wherever he lived, Ron became connected to the local Jewish community. In Asheville, Ron developed programs for and led the Center for Jewish Studies (CJS) at UNC Asheville as steering council chair. CJS is an organization that connects the Jewish community with the campus. Ron is pictured in 1966 in Coldwater, Michigan.

Ron has published numerous studies investigating philosophical issues of later life and human development. Some of his books have been translated into Chinese and Korean. Ron's first published book was *Kierkegaard As Educator* (University of California Press, 1977). When Ron edited the *Older Americans Almanac*, he collaborated with NCCCR participants.

Articles in publications such as The *New York Times* gave NCCCR national recognition. The cover of *Parade* magazine brought the world to NCCCR. Six thousand letters poured in requesting information about the programs by people who wanted to participate and people who wanted to see centers modeled after NCCCR in their locations.

This interpretive panel located at:
The Reuter Center, Manheimer room, Osher Lifelong Learning Institute.
Phone: (828) 251-6140
www.olliasheville.com

Photos courtesy of Ronald Manheimer and OLLI. Photos of Ron with mountains in the background and Ron and Rick Moody taken by Gail Manheimer. Additional information about Ron can be found at D. Hiden Ramsey Library, Special Collections UNC Asheville.

Some people in this chapter you might have heard about, some you might remember, and some you might know as people still in our midst. Some have left reminders, some might surprise you, and some are up and coming.

Looking Back

Sir Phillip Henry was an Australian Jew who made a fortune in copper and coffee before moving to the

Thomas Wolfe referred to Zelandia as the "rich Jew's castle on top of Birdseye" in *Look Homeward, Angel*. The estate had a bridge that Wolfe called "rich Jew Phillip Roseberry's bridge." Today it is known as Helen's bridge. (Courtesy of Pack Library, North Carolina Collection)

A festive gathering at Zelandia shows people in costume. Sir Philip Henry is at the far right, next to Edith (Mrs. George) Vanderbilt who is wearing a hat with seven stars suspended on a wire above it, and star earrings. 1920s (Courtesy of Pack Library, North Carolina Collection)

United States in 1900. Internationally known, he served as a board member of the Jewish Theological Seminary. In 1903, after his wife's tragic death in a fire in their New York home, he purchased the Zelandia estate, a three-story, sixty-two-room Tudor-style English manor house with a separate cottage and stables, atop Beaucatcher Mountain. Sir Phillip lived there until his death in 1933.

An avid book collector, Henry purchased a rare 1616 manuscript of Hapsburg history that he returned to the Emperor Franz Joseph of Austria. This gesture earned him the title of Commander of the Order of Franz Josef, conferred upon him by the Emperor himself. Locally, Henry donated funds for CBHT to remove the steeple from its first building on Market Street, which had formerly been a church.

Leo Cadison (1901-1975) and **Lou Pollock** (1887-1959) were friends from Pittsburgh. They arrived together in Asheville around 1913 as traveling salesmen. Leo became involved in the Jewish community, serving as president of the West Asheville Hebrew Cemetery Association and on the Bikur Cholim auditing committee. He eventually worked as a political operative for Supreme Court Justice Tom Clark, and ironically, for Senator Robert R. Reynolds, who had a reputation for being an anti-Semite. (Senator Reynolds also socialized with the Pollocks despite his reputation.) Leo later went

Perhaps Henry's most lasting contribution to Asheville was the founding of the Asheville Art Association and Museum in 1930, where he displayed his own extensive art collection in one of Zelandia's buildings. (That building was later demolished when Interstate 240 was cut through Beaucatcher Mountain.) A small part of Henry's collection was later incorporated into the Asheville Art Museum. (Courtesy of Pack Library, North Carolina Collection)

Lou Pollock, president of both CBHT and CBI congregations, owned several shoe stores and held a yearly shoe giveaway for needy children. The West Asheville Hebrew Cemetery Association renamed their burial ground Lou Pollock Memorial Park to honor his involvement. (Courtesy of Ramsey Library Special Collections)

on to work for the Justice Department and became public relations director of the National Conference on Citizenship.

Though he traveled widely, Dan kept his connection to Asheville, referring to it as the finest city in the country in which to live! 1930s (Courtesy of Ken Michalove)

Dan Michalove's (1893-1949) roots were in the Jewish community of Asheville. His father was S.H. Michalove, owner of the IXL store on Haywood Street, which sold fine china and glassware. Dan began his career as the manager of an Asheville movie theater and worked his way up to Vice President of Twentieth Century Fox Film Corporation. Along the way, he also owned an Atlanta baseball club, the Crackers, and built Western North Carolina's first drive-in theater on Hendersonville Road in Arden with his brother-in-law, Charles Roth.

Several other members of the Jewish community were involved in the early days of Asheville's movie and broadcasting scene. **David Schandler** and a partner built the Pack Theater, which later became the Plaza Theater, at 2 Biltmore Avenue. This theater closed just prior to the Great Depression in 1928 or 1929. **Lewis Blomberg** opened the Strand Theater on Patton Avenue between 1917 and 1919.

The Wolfson family of Miami, Florida had an estate in Asheville in the Beaverdam area. Their company, Wometco Enterprises, owned and purchased WLOS-WKJV -WWNC- WKSF AM/FM/TV in Asheville in 1958. They promptly sold the AM station, but operated both the television and FM stations as Wometco Skyway Broadcasting until 1984. According to Rob Neufeld, columnist for the *Asheville Citizen Times*, **Mitchell Wolfson, Sr.** created the Beaver Lake Country Club, which was purchased by the Asheville Country Club after they sold their original course to the Grove Park Inn. Jackie Gleason would come up to Asheville to visit Mitchell, Sr. and golf on his course. The Wolfsons donated a modern sculpture that still stands by Beaver Lake. **Mitchell Wolfson, Jr.** lived in Asheville when he was a teenager. Here he read Thomas Wolfe, which sparked his curiosity to learn about everything. This led him to a life of collecting cultural objects that now fill the Wolfsonian Museum in Miami Beach, Florida.

Connie Lerner was crowned "Miss Asheville" in 1970 and became "Miss North Carolina" later that year. She was the only Jewish Miss North Carolina to date. A gifted pianist, Connie played Chopin's Revolutionary Etude for the talent competition. This piece held special significance for her, and her parents, who were Holocaust survivors as it had been played in defiance of the German occupation of Poland in 1939. Connie won the state swimsuit competition and was a talent winner in the Miss America pageant. She is included in Frank Deford's bestseller *There She is: The Life and Times of Miss America* and in Eli Evans' book *The Lonely Days were Sundays*.

Connie Lerner sharing her Miss North Carolina crown. (Courtesy of Wake Forest Medical School, Dorothy Carpenter Medical Archives)

LeRoy Gross took over his father's jewelry store, Carolina Jewelers on Patton Avenue in the late 1950s, but it was not his life's calling. He wanted to follow his passion, the stock market. So, in 1963 he moved to Charlotte and by 1970 he was recruited by Wall Street when they noticed his success. LeRoy brought his options sales strategies to Reynolds, Inc, a stock brokerage that later merged with Dean Witter. They offered him $100,000 a year which he turned down for $36,000 and 1% of his options sales. He went on to write six books, teach and retire early unfortunately passing away at age 60 in 1988.

Robert (Bob) Moog was a creative genius who revolutionized the world of electronic music. He started his first business, manufacturing Theremin kits, at age 19 in New York. The Theremin, invented by Leon Theremin, created sound which the performer controlled without physically contacting the instrument. Moog's company's sales paid his way through college, where he earned degrees in physics, electrical engineering, and a Ph.D. in engineering physics. Bob developed and refined his own line of modular synthesizer systems, and formed R.A. Moog Company in 1967. He moved to Asheville in 1978, restarting his manufacturing company, today known as Moog Music, Inc. In the early 1990s, he was a research professor of music at UNC Asheville. He received a Grammy Trustees Award for lifetime achievement in 1970 and in 2002 was honored with a Special Merit/ Technical Grammy Award. Sadly, he was diagnosed with a brain tumor and died at the age of 71. He

Robert Moog (1934-2005) created a modular electronic synthesizer that had a keyboard and was compact enough to be easily portable. His instruments were first used in 1950's sci-fi thrillers. They went on to revolutionize rock, as some of the top bands, from the Beatles to Emerson Lake & Palmer, to Sting and the Police used synthesizers. Later he created an effects pedal known as a Moogerfooger. (Courtesy of Moog Music Inc.)

is buried in Lou Pollock Memorial Park. The Bob Moog Foundation was created as a memorial to him and continues his life's work of developing electronic music.

Jack Benatan was born in 1919 in Cape Town, South Africa. He was educated there and served

Wedding of Jack and Nikki Reidbord Benatan, Tel Aviv, Israel June 1949, just after Israel's first birthday. Robert Capa, a *Life* and *Look* photographer who came with friends, took the photo. Nikki and Jack had each been enlisted in the Israeli army for the past year. (Courtesy of Nikki Benatan)

in the South African Army during World War II. In 1948, he enlisted in the Israeli Army, where he fought in Israel's War of Independence. There he also met and married his American wife, Nicki, of Pittsburgh, Pennsylvania. She was serving in the Israeli army as a nurse. Jack came with Nikki to the United States in 1949 and became a U.S. Citizen in 1960. He and Nikki shared their stories of adventure during the Israeli war and were active in the Jewish community and the Center for Creative Retirement (now the Osher Life Long Learning Institute or OLLI) where they introduced lawn bowling.

In Our Midst

Eli Evans, author and son of the Mayor of Durham during the 1960s, remarked, "Jews in the South work for a larger community because they know a better community for everybody is better for them and their children." Many of today's Jewish Ashevillians continue to positively impact the larger community. Here we name only some of the many talented and inspiring people who follow in the footsteps of a long line of Jews who have helped us to define ourselves, brought our Jewish community together to find our voices, and helped to make a difference. Each day becomes tomorrow's history.

Asheville's Jewish Mayors

Kenneth (Ken) Michalove, whose ancestors came to Asheville in the 1880s, spent most of his career in service to the community, beginning in the early 1960s with the anti-poverty programs

Kenneth Michalove has been a part of many changes, serving as the City Manager, member of City Council, and then Mayor of Asheville (1989-1993). He also worked for St. Joseph's Hospital.

of the Opportunity Corporation, Model Cities, and the Housing Authority. He continued his government service in the early '70s as City/County liaison, Assistant City Manager, City Manager, Council Member, and Mayor, ending in the early 1990s. From there he spent 18 years as an executive with St. Joseph's Health Services Corporation. Ken also did volunteer service on numerous local, regional, and statewide boards and commissions; and, in most cases, he was elected to roles as an officer with those organizations. He was JCC President in 1968

While Ken was Mayor, the Ku Klux Klan applied for a permit to hold a march. On the same day, the Klan also applied for a permit in Hendersonville, where Ken's cousin, Don Michalove, was the Mayor. Paul Michalove, another cousin, recalls that the Klan, after receiving their permits, asked if all Jewish mayors were named Michalove!

Mayor Leni Sitnik gave The Key To The City to Sir Elton John

When **Leni Sitnick** became Asheville's first female Mayor (1997-2001), she opened the doors and windows of City Hall. Her goal was to be an elected official who was accessible and transparent. As Mayor, she created an environment for comfortable public participation and insisted that every citizen be heard at City Council meetings,

so meetings often ran late into the night. Leni often talked to school children. She would tell them what her mother and father always told her: "If you work hard, stay in school, listen to your teachers and believe in yourself, you can be anything you want to be." By the end of her talk, the children could repeat these words by heart. Prior to taking office, Leni was a community activist and leader.

Esther Manheimer lights the menorah at The Chabad House annual Chanukah Live celebration (Courtesy of The Chabad House of Asheville)

Esther Manheimer moved to Asheville with her family as a teenager, when her father became the head of the Center for Creative Retirement. Esther was elected to the Asheville City Council in 2009, and became Mayor in 2013. As a practicing attorney, Esther has received much recognition, including General Federation of Women's Clubs of North Carolina's "Women of Achievement Award," North Carolina Lawyers Weekly's "Leaders in the Law," Pisgah Legal Services' "Most Valuable Mountain Area Volunteer Lawyer," and YWCA of Asheville's "Tribute to Women of Influence (TWIN) Award." Esther worked at the JCC as a lifeguard in her teens and later served on the Board becoming President in 2007.

Law and Order

What Jewish mother does not brag about their son or daughter the lawyer? There have been many Jewish Ashevillians in the field of law who would make their mothers "kvell."

Barry Schochet, whose family, the Blombergs, arrived in Asheville in the 1880s, served on the Senate Watergate committee and was visible every day when the hearings were televised for 250 hours between May 17th and August 7th, 1973. He wrote the questions asked by Senator Herman Talmadge (D-GA).

The North Carolina Bar Association honors a member of each Judicial District for outstanding service that benefits the local community and exemplifies the highest standards of professionalism. This honor has been bestowed upon several outstanding members of the Jewish community, including **Kerry Friedman** (2002), **Bob Deutsch** (2009), and **Judge Dennis Winner** (2010). **Hank Teich** was on the list of North Carolina Super Lawyers for 5 years and served for 20 years as a Public Guardian representing incompetent adults and mentally disabled Veterans. Other members of the legal profession have been recognized, including **Harris M. Livingstain**, who was named to the 2015 Super Lawyers List in estate and probate, and **Sabrina Presnell Rockoff** for employment and labor law.

Dennis Winner became a District Court Judge at the age of 28 in 1970. By 1972, he was appointed to the Superior Court where he served for three years. He became a Superior Court Judge again

Leslie and Dennis Winner were the first brother and sister to be elected to the North Carolina Senate at the same time. (Courtesy of Leslie Winner)

in 1994, when he was appointed by then Governor Jim Hunt. When his appointment ended, he was elected into the position in 1996 and 2004. Between his judgeships, Dennis practiced law for 19 years in Asheville and served six terms in the state Senate. "Next to my family, public service has been the most important thing in my life," he said.

Leslie Winner, has also spent much of her career as a public servant and public interest lawyer working on issues such as civil rights, gender equity, affordable housing, public education and higher education. Leslie served as general counsel to the Charlotte-Mecklenburg Board of Education and as Vice President and General Counsel to the University of North Carolina. She was elected to three terms (1993-1998) with the North Carolina State Senate. In 2008, Leslie became the Executive Director of the Z. Smith Reynolds Foundation.

Kerry Friedman started practicing law in 1980 with a focus in business, transactional and non-

profit law. Besides the 2001 Centennial Award presented by the North Carolina Bar Association and 28th Judicial District Bar, Kerry has been named by Business North Carolina Magazine as one of their "Legal Elite," in 2013, 2014 and 2015. Kerry has given tirelessly of his time and service not only to the Jewish community, but also to the wider Asheville non-profit community. He

Kerry Friedman, an Asheville native, left town only long enough to attend college and law school. (Courtesy of Kerry Friedman)

has served on numerous boards, including the UNC Asheville Foundation, United Way of Asheville-Buncombe County, Community Foundation of Western North Carolina, Care Partners Foundation, Pisgah Legal Services, and many other community organizations. From 1992-1994 Kerry served as JCC President. Is there a nonprofit in town that has not had Kerry on its board?

Frank Goldsmith's professional choices have always been guided by his commitment to Judaism's *gemilut chasidim* (deeds of loving kindness), which enable him to help others. He has worked tirelessly for the rights of those who are often ignored, concentrating on civil rights and other civil matters. He was part of the legal team that worked with the Southern Poverty Law Center to eliminate a Neo-Nazi group in Swain County. His pro bono work has included representing death row

Frank Goldsmith has followed his passion in the study of law, multiple languages, martial arts, hiking, flying, certification as an Emergency Medical Technician and Judaism (Courtesy of Lee Avishai)

inmates and Guantanamo detainees (2007 – 2014). In a *Time* op-ed, Frank was asked to write about his defense of five Guantanamo detainees all of whom are now free. He said, "I am an American lawyer who believes that even the most despised person – perhaps especially the most despised person – has the right to a vigorous defense."

Frank's work in mediation reflects his continued commitment to seeking fair compromise and establishing trusting relationships among adversaries. It earned him the American Civil Liberties Union's Frank Porter Graham Award in 1987 and the North Carolina Human Rights Coalition's International Human Rights Award in 2011. Frank was one of five attorneys profiled in a 1999 series of articles in *The North Carolina State Bar Journal* entitled *Searching for Atticus Finch*. He has been named to the Best Lawyers in America, the North Carolina Legal Elite and the North Carolina Super Lawyers. Currently, he is a Board of Directors member of the NC Justice Center and Carolina Public Press. Judy Leavitt, a fellow member of the Carolina Jews for Justice-WNC Chapter, sums it up: "Frank lives the life of *Tikkun Elam* in every way. His quest for justice is the core of who he is." In addition to his accomplishments, Frank served as the President of CBI from 1998-2000.

Robert Deutsch has been practicing law for more than forty years. In November 2013, Bob was selected

to be the attorney for the Buncombe County Board of Commissioners. Governor Jim Hunt appointed Bob to serve on the Board of Directors of the North Carolina-Israel Partnership. He is also on the Board of Directors of the American-Israel Chamber of Commerce, Southeast, and the advisory board of Tel Aviv University Recanati School of Management. In addition, Bob served as the President of CBI from 1990-1992. His wife, **Carol Deutsch** has been involved with Jewish youth serving as Bet Sefer Principal at CBI, establishing Woven Youth, a

Bob and Carol Deutsch have been very involved with the local and national Jewish community. Every year, they sponsor programs with several of Asheville's Jewish organizations including the CJS, JCC, CBI and CBHT.

community wide teen group at the JCC and a Youth Advisory Board, which lead to affiliating with Young Judea, a national youth organization. Carol, has also served on the Boards of Directors for the Asheville Art Museum, Chamber of Commerce, Diana Wortham Theatre, The Community Foundation of WNC, Women Mean Business and WCQS.

Marc Rudow specializes in bankruptcy and real estate law, for which he has won many awards. He is actively involved with the NC Conservancy Trust and Pisgah Legal Services, and he teaches at South College. The Best Lawyers in America named him 2015 Lawyer of the Year in Asheville for Real Estate Law. The North Carolina Bar Association gave him their Citizen Lawyer Award in 2012. Marc is also a talented musician and a founding member of the Bandana Klezmer band. Marc was a lifeguard at the JCC in his teens and later served as President from 1998 to 1999.

Following a workshop taught by Andy John at the JCC in 2005, Marc's band, Bandana Klezmer, was formed. Since then, they have built a repertoire that includes hundreds of tunes; and over the years, they have brought the music of our Eastern European ancestors to the people of Western North Carolina through numerous celebrations, festivals and concerts. Members of the band, from front to back: **Meg Peterson, accordion, Rob Levin, guitar, Andy John, cello and harmonica, Michael Hunt, tsimbl and poyk, Marc Rudow, fiddle, Naomi Dalglish, fiddle (Courtesy of Wanda Levin)**

Performing Arts

Daliah Gans appeared in the films Lord Jim (1965), The Spy with a Cold Nose (1966), Casino Royale (1967), and Catlow (1971) with Yul Brynner.

Daliah Gans lives a quiet life in Asheville; but beyond our borders, particularly in Germany, she is a well-known and much beloved singer. Born in Israel, Daliah Lavi (her professional name) was a star in Europe before she made her Hollywood debut. She began training as a dancer and actor before she abruptly halted her career to serve in the Israeli army. In the early 1960s, she returned to acting.

Students preparing for their B'nai Mitzvah at Congregation Beth Israel were not born yet when their teacher, **Josefa Briant**, danced in the movie, *Jesus Christ Superstar*. They may not know she was born on Kibbutz Yagur in Israel, and became a soloist in Israel's famed Bat Sheva Dance Company. In New York, she worked as a dancer with Merce Cunningham and Maggie Black, and as an assistant choreographer at Alvin Ailey American Dance Theater. Now residing in Asheville, Josefa has shared her talents with our community through creative movement classes for pre-school children and teaching Hebrew and Kabbalah at UNC Asheville.

Noah began playing violin at age four. At age nine, he played for Lord Yehudi Menuhin in Switzerland. (Courtesy of Noah Bendix Balgley)

Noah Bendix Balgley (b.1984) has thrilled and moved audiences around the world with his violin performances. While doing genealogical research, Noah's mother, Meredith Balgley, discovered that her grandfather, Samuel Leventhal, had studied violin in Berlin, played with the Pittsburgh Symphony in the early 1900s, joined the Victor Herbert Orchestra, and later was Concertmaster of the Hartford Symphony.

Noah became the concertmaster of the Pittsburgh Symphony and is currently first Concertmaster of the Berlin Philharmonic. At the Pittsburgh Pirates Opening Day at PNC Park in 2012, Noah performed his own version of the *Star-Spangled Banner* for solo violin in front of 39,000 fans. In his spare time, Noah enjoys playing Klezmer music, performing with world-renowned Klezmer groups such as Brave Old World, and teaching klezmer violin at workshops in Europe and in the United States. He performs on a Cremonese violin made in 1732 by Carlo Bergonzi.

Erik Bendix, Noah's father, began folk dancing in Europe at age 10 and has now been a major teacher of international folk dance for 26 years, including traditions as diverse as Macedonian and clogging. Since 1991, he has co-taught traditional Yiddish dance with Brave Old World, introducing it to wider audiences. He is known for his user-friendly teaching and his attention to style.

Robin Jane Feld (1949-2004), a member of the Lipinsky family, grew up in Asheville. She was an internationally known performer and teacher of contact improvisation, an art form inspired by ballet and jazz. Along with her husband, Paul McCandless, the Grammy-award winning musician and reed instrumentalist, she and a group of young performers at Full Circle residential treatment center in Bolinas, California recorded a CD titled *Taking Flight*.

Theme composer **BJ Leiderman** spent his summers at Camp Blue Star in Hendersonville growing up. In 2011 he had a vortex experience which drew him back to the mountains of WNC. BJ has worked as a writer (as in "copywriter") for clients as diverse as Nickelodeon, The Chris Rock Show, Fox Kids, Cartoon Network, Christian Broadcasting Network, and Spike TV and written the theme music for a variety of Public Radio shows including *Morning Edition, Weekend Edition, Marketplace, Wait, Wait, Don't Tell Me* and *Car Talk* winning numerous awards. He is currently working on a cd of original music.

Eliot performs locally with world fusion trio Free Planet Radio and the Asheville Symphony where he plays the bass. He has also played with the Paul Winter Consort, composer Paul Halley, pianist/humorist Steve Allen, and the Cab Calloway Big Band, to name a few.

A professional musician since 1977, **Eliot Wadopian** loves to explore all music styles from jazz, rock, blues, country, and folk to symphonic classical, opera and ethnic styles from India, the Middle East, Latin America and Eastern Europe. He is one of those extraordinary musicians who shares his lifetime of varied musical experiences through his performances, teaching and well over 100 recordings. Eliot is a two-time Grammy Award winner (1993) as a member of the Paul Winter Ensemble. He grew up in Asheville, where his father was a partner in the Vanderbilt Shirt Factory. He still calls this city home.

Steven Heller is a three-time Grammy award-winning producer-composer. (Courtesy of Steven and Maggie Heller)

Steven Heller is a modest man. He does not talk about the fact that his work has been featured in recordings, live concerts, television and movie scores, including the Miramax movie *The Journey of August King,* and music for the Animal Planet Network. Steven has been awarded several Telly and Addy Awards for television and radio commercial music compositions; and he has received national recognition, including three American Library Association's Notable Children's Recording Awards, and various Parents' Choice Awards. Two Grammy Awards were for the production of David Holt's *Stellaluna* (1997) and the engineering and production of the album *Legacy,* featuring Doc Watson and David Holt (2003). Throughout his career, Heller has continued to donate his services for campaigns to protect the local environment and to benefit our Western North Carolina community, including Southern Appalachian Forest Coalition, Southwings, the Blue Ridge Parkway, United Way, Professional Parenting (foster care for children), Manna Food Bank and more.

Steven's parents, Max and Trude Heller, escaped from Nazi-occupied Vienna, Austria and settled in Greenville, South Carolina. After retiring from a career in business, Max became Greenville's Mayor from 1971 until 1979, and later the Chair of the South Carolina State Development Board. Two of Steven and Maggie Heller's sons continue the music legacy. **Elliot Heller** is New York-based DJ Equal, and **Drew Heller** is a member of the world music group Toubab Krewe.

Billy Jonas has been a gift to Asheville's music scene since he moved here in 1991. His talent enhances services at CBHT as part of the sacred music team, and his concerts of original music enthrall young and old alike. His CD, *What Kind of Cat are You?!* received First Place/Gold from the American Federation of Independent Musicians and a Parents' Choice Gold Award. Billy's videos

In 2010, Billy Jonas and the Billy Jonas Band were invited to perform at the White House, as well as at the John F. Kennedy Center for the Performing Arts. (Courtesy billyjonas.com)

have garnered multiple accolades, including Parents' Choice Awards and a *New York Times* "Best for Kids" listing.

Ira Bernstein describes himself as a percussive step dancer who specializes in Appalachian flatfooting. He was a boy from Long Island, New York who graduated from the University of Pennsylvania and turned down an opportunity to become a veterinarian to study dance. Ira has performed all over the world doing clogging, flatfoot and step dancing as well a tap. Among his many awards he has repeatedly won first place in the Mount Airy Fiddler's Convention old-time flatfooting competition. On television and in theatrical productions, Ira has performed with the world's greatest tap and step dancers, including Gregory Hines, Savion Glover, Honi Coles, Jimmy Slyde, and Chuck Green. One of the artistic creators and featured soloists in Mountain Legacy of Asheville, Ira is also the director of the Ten Toe Percussion Ensemble, a collective of internationally acclaimed step dance soloists, as well as the originator of the Festival of Percussive Dance. Besides dancing, Ira plays the fiddle—though he is not the first in his family. Several of his Ashkenazi ancestors played the violin in Europe.

Ira Bernstein has been described as having mercurial feet and rhythmic virtuosity. He was drawn to the Appalachian heritage of Western North Carolina and served as the music coordinator of the Montford Music and Arts Festival for several years. (Courtesy Hobart Jones)

Telling Our Stories

The Rudow family has been a part of the JCC for two generations. From left to right: Deborah Miles, Marc Rudow, Josh Rudow, Caleb Rudow, and David Rudow (Courtesy of Deborah Miles)

Deborah Miles founded the Center for Diversity Education at the Asheville JCC in 1995. Today the organization is known as Center for Diversity at Education UNC Asheville, and its goal is celebrating and teaching diversity in order to foster conversation and respect among cultures. The Center's vision is to build relationships across differences to create a more inclusive and equitable community. Programming efforts are directed at local schools, university students, faculty and staff and the broader community. Its many local and traveling exhibits have brought awareness and knowledge to thousands of schoolchildren. In 2005, Deborah received the prestigious Nancy Susan Reynolds Award for race relations from the Z. Smith Reynolds Foundation.

Another of Center for Diversity Education at UNC Asheville projects was *From the Shoah to the Mountains*, which recorded testimonies of local Holocaust survivors. Theirs is the hardest kind of celebrity as survivors of genocide. These interviews are kept in the Jewish Life in Western North Carolina Collection at UNC Asheville Ramsey Library Special Collections and are available online.

Dr. Eric Wellisch, of blessed memory, passed away on July 9, 2015 at the age of 94. Eric led an epic life, which began in the area of Austria where his family had lived for countless generations. The Wellischs were, however, the only Jewish family in their town of Weisenfeld. Everyone there lived in harmony, so much so that the sheriff almost apologized when he took Eric and his father to jail on Kristallnacht, November 11, 1938. This was the moment when Eric resolved to join a cousin in America. Once safely in the Asheville, Eric had the *chutzpa* (nerve) to write directly to President Roosevelt and ask him to help bring his parents and sister to safety. Steve Early, Roosevelt's Press Secretary, replied; and within months, the family was reunited.

Dedicated in 2015, this monument is in the town of Wiesenfeld, Austria where Eric lived as a child. It reads: "The Jewish merchant family of Hugo Wellisch lived in this house. In 1939, they were expelled by the Nazis from their homeland. Never Again!"

Eric joined the 44th Combat Engineering Battalion of the American Army in 1944, a few days into the Normandy Invasion. In May of 1945, Eric and his fellow soldiers stopped in Buchenwald death camp and saw firsthand the horrors. When Eric returned to the United States, he enrolled in Columbia, and later Purdue University, earning a doctorate in 1951. He came to Asheville in 1964, where he worked for Olin and Ecusta in Brevard. Eric served as JCC President from 1971 to 72. Despite his trials, Eric saw no obstacles or challenges, only opportunities.

Eric was a longtime volunteer and supporter of UNC Asheville's Center for Diversity Education at UNC Asheville. He shared his story in countless schools and always charmed the students and teachers while impressing on them that the seeds of prejudice are always among us; and it is up to each of us whether these seeds will be allowed to grow. Dr. Wellisch represented the generation of memory that witnessed and survived the Holocaust and leaves a generation of students to carry the stories, and their lessons, forward.

Walter retired as an emeritus professor from Mars Hill University and continues to teach at area colleges and in elder hostels throughout the country, often sharing his experiences as a survivor of one of the world's worst atrocities. (Courtesy of Ramsey Library Special Collections)

Dr. Walter Ziffer was born in 1926 in Ceske Tesin, Czech Republic, following a long line of ancestors that go back at least 400 years. He survived a series of labor camps from 1942 to 1945 and was finally liberated by the Soviet Army from Grosse Rosen. Walter later immigrated to the United States. After earning an engineering degree and working six years for General Motors, he returned to school to obtain three additional degrees, including a Ph.D., and became a professor of theology in the United States and in France.

Lotte Strauss Meyerson grew up in Darmstad, Germany, where her family operated a textile business. As the Nazis gained power, they were forced to sell their business at a deep discount to their employees. They had cousins in New York who were willing to sponsor only her father to come to America. It took him six months to bring his family to Chicago, where they settled. At sixteen, Lotte attended a gathering for young immigrants. Someone there invited her to the Hyde Park Co-Op Youth League meetings that took place

Lotte (r) and Seymour (l) were instrumental, with their daughter Elana, in founding Westwood Cohousing Community, an intentional community of 24 homes in West Asheville, which brought them here in 1997. Lotte served two years as its President.

each Saturday night. The format began with a serious discussion topic and ended with international folk dancing.

Lotte's intellectual life and her commitment to social justice were formed during the years of persecution in Germany and informed by the experience of the Co-Op Youth League where she met others who were thinking of serious matters. It was at the Youth League that she met Seymour, whom she married in 1943, just before he went into the army. He was sent to Germany just as the war ended and sent home reports of Darmstadt, which was 80% destroyed. Seymour was a chemist who worked for Standard Oil doing mass spectrometry research and development.

Lotte was the chair of the Social Justice Committee at CBHT and a speaker on the Holocaust to classrooms of students. She is active in the ACLU and World Federalist Association. The WNC Chapter of the ACLU presented its annual Evan Mahaney Champion of Civil Liberties Award in 2011 to Lotte.

Fine Arts

According to Pam Myers, "Museums are places of inspiration and gathering; places that honor the maker and that explore creativity. They are havens where all kinds of dialogue can happen."

Pamela Myers (Pam) has been at the helm of the Asheville Art Museum since 1995. She has brought several Jewish-themed exhibits to the museum, which exposed viewers to different perspectives on the Jewish community. She feels that it is not an accident that so many leaders of nonprofit organizations are Jewish. **David Whitehill**, Executive Director of the Asheville Symphony is one of these leaders. Much Jewish thought is given to the commitment to create a better community for all.

Norman Sultan (1917-1981), the owner of Carolina Tire, was known as the "Sultan of Tires," But on

Phyllis and Norman Sultan were interested in the arts. They brought their four children up to follow their passions. Left to right: Donald, Nancy, Terrie and Jeffrey in front and Phyllis and Norman in the back, late 1960s (Courtesy of Phyllis Sultan)

Sunday, he was an abstract painter. **Phyllis Sultan**, whose father owned Galumbeck and Company on Broadway, actively pursued theatre. **Donald Sultan** (b. 1951) is a renowned painter, sculptor and printmaker, who incorporates industrial materials such as tar, enamel, spackle and vinyl tiles into some of his pieces. His works have been exhibited internationally in prominent museums and galleries, and are included in important museum collections all over the globe. Daughter **Nancy Sultan** is a professor of Greek and Roman Studies, another daughter **Terrie Sultan** is the Director of the Parrish Art Museum in Water Mill, New York, and son **Jeffrey Sultan** is an engineer.

Families like the Sultans exemplify a change from one generation to the next. Often children of the immigrant generation had to follow into their family's business for economic reasons especially during the Great Depression. But they were able to encourage their own children to be what they wanted to be and follow their dreams

Throughout 2014, Benjamin Betsalel met with the family members of persons who went missing in the armed conflict on November 13th, 2014 in Bogotá, creating a series of portraits of the family members, which also includes short narratives and objects of remembrance. This is meant to highlight the needs of family members of people who disappear. *Man With a Past*, 2009 (Courtesy of Benjamin Betsalel)

Benjamin Betsalel came to live in Asheville when he was nine years old. While in high school one of his portraits won a national American Visions award and was shown at the Corcoran Gallery in Washington DC in 1999. He went on to study at the Savanah College of Art and Design, University of Chester (in England and UNC Asheville. His works have deep and thoughtful meanings. … and survivors of conflict. He now paints and shows his work internationally.

He once created a 9-panel, 24-foot long mixed media piece and research presentation on German-Jewish poet Nelly Sachs: *Visualizing Humanities: painting in response to the poetry and life of Nelly Sachs*, which was presented at the 2004 National Conference on Undergraduate Research in Indianapolis, Indiana. This project focused on personal versus perceived identity, the death and rebirth of language, and the inherent tensions faced by displaced people and survivors of conflict.

Other artistic local notables include: **Alex Bernstein** whose exquisite glass sculptures have been exhibited in the United States and Europe. **Darren Green** whose work with recycled wood and environmentally friendly finishes has been noticed in a myriad of magazines nationally and internationally. His amazing business, the Old Wood Company prides itself on its craftsmanship and sustainability. **Ami James**, Israeli-American celebrity tattoo artist whose creative designs could make anyone want a tattoo. Check their websites and you can see for yourself.

The Written Word

Richard (Rick) Chess is the kind of teacher who students later remember as being the inspiration for them to follow their dreams. His teaching awards are numerous. Rick is the Director of the Center for Jewish Studies (since 1992) at UNC Asheville, bringing some of the most important Jewish scholars of our time to speak and interact with students. He is also advisor to the campus Hillel.

In addition to teaching at UNC Asheville, Rick Chess has served as a faculty member at the Jewish Arts Institute, Isabella Freedman Retreat Center, the Brandeis Bardin Institute, and the Bread Loaf School of English. (Courtesy of Rick Chess)

Eternally a poet, Rick is the author of three books: *Third Temple, Chair in the Desert* and *Tekiah*. His poems appear in a number of anthologies, including *Telling and Remembering: A Century of American Jewish Poetry* and *The Bloomsbury Anthology of Contemporary American Jewish Poetry*. Rick has been a contributing editor to *ZEEK: A Jewish Journal of Thought and Culture*, and had essays published in *Image: A Journal of Art, Faith and Mystery*. He regularly contributes to the blog *Good Letters*, and his poem "Kaddish" was included in *Best American Spiritual Writing 2005*.

Lauren Rosenfeld is not only the Director of CBHT's religious school, but is also a self-proclaimed professional "soul declutterer." Her spiritual drive to help people organize their lives and let go of physical and emotional clutter has led her to co-author two books: *Your To Be List: Turn Those Dreaded To-Do's Into Meaningful Moments Every Day*, written with her husband, James McMahon, and *Breathing Room, Open Your Heart by Decluttering Your Home*, co-authored with Dr. Melva Green.

Miranda Richmond Mouillot is the daughter of Ileana Grams Moog and stepdaughter of Robert Moog. Ileana is a retired philosophy professor at UNC Asheville and a former director of the Center for Jewish Studies at the university. Miranda, an Asheville native, published a book entitled: *A Fifty-Year Silence: Love, War, and a Ruined House in France*. It chronicles her journey to find out what happened in her grandparents' relationship that tore them apart after they survived World War II in Europe.

Miranda Richmond Mouillot's book illustrates how strongly generations are connected. The trauma of genocide not only affects the people who lived through the experience, but their descendants who must continue to tell the story. (Courtesy of Sharon Fahrer)

Charles Gershon served as President of CBHT 2003-2005 (Courtesy of Ramsey Library Special Collections)

Charles Gershon came to Asheville after practicing urology in Atlanta for many years. As a Diplomat of the American Board of Urology and a Fellow of the American College of Surgeons, he wrote fifteen scientific papers and presented at numerous medical conferences. In Asheville, Charles reinvented himself and began a career as a novelist. His novels to date are *The Hydrangea People* and *Slow Funeral*.

David Schulman grew up in Sylva, North Carolina, where his father Sol Schulman ran a clothing store for 70 years. Sylva did not have its own synagogue, so David's family belonged to CBI. In the early 1990s,

David interviewed several senior members of the Jewish community, realizing if their stories were not recorded, they would soon be lost. The transcripts of those interviews are in the Jewish Life in Western North Carolina collection at UNC Asheville. More recently, David wrote a murder mystery about an event that took place at the Battery Park Hotel, entitled *The Past is Never Dead*. Its main character's name is Gritz Goldberg.

More to Kvell About

Asheville has long been home to many outstanding doctors, including Sprinza Weizenblatt and Samuel Robinson. More recently, **Dr. Alan Baumgarten** has received wide recognition for many accomplishments, including his work with family centered medical homes. He is the founder of the Nutrition Support Team at Mission Hospital, where he trained medical students, resident physicians and medical staff physicians on the benefits of nutrition in patient care, recovery and illness prevention.

In April of 2009, doctors Jonas and Meryl Goldstein got their kids up on stage for their first musical performance as the Goldstein Family Band. Since then, the band has performed for dozens of live audiences. Playing a mix of Israeli, Yiddish and Rock 'n' Roll classics, their fun and eclectic show includes lyrics in five languages.

The Goldstein family is close knit. Robert and Leslie, along with their three sons and daughters-in-law, all settled in Asheville, where they are now raising their families. The adult Goldsteins are outstanding professionals in their fields, including medicine, law and real estate. In addition, they are all active participants in Asheville's Jewish community. **Heather Whittaker Goldstein**, who now practices law, was the Executive Director of the JCC from 2003 to 2012.

Patti Glazer has been the architect for a remarkable number of Asheville building renovation projects. Her interests are wide-ranging. She went to high school in Mexico, was a Fulbright scholar who studied tapestry making in Poland, and has amassed a large collection of hand-made craft mugs and earrings. (Courtesy of Patti Glazer)

Patti Glazer, known as the "Building Code Queen" for her ability to figure out the best way to achieve code compliance, has left her mark on the architectural fabric of Asheville and has won many awards for her prowess. Patti designed the JCC building. Jan Schochet a friend of Patti since Patti moved to Asheville in 1980, said, "I've watched as she's gone from a new architect, to a founding partner in the first women's-owned architecture firm in western NC, to owner of her own firm."

Patti's father was Joe Glazer a union organizer known as "Labor's Troubadour"

Steven L. Solnick and his family are relative newcomers to Asheville. After a decade abroad as the Ford Foundation's representative in Moscow and then in New Delhi, Steven was installed as the seventh President of Warren Wilson College in 2012. Steven is a member of CBHT, where he has spoken about his overseas experiences in promoting human rights, higher education, arts and culture, media, sustainable agriculture and reproductive health.

Lenny Bernstein was part of the Intergovernmental Panel on Climate Change (IPCC) that, along with Al Gore, won the 2007 Nobel Peace Prize. His wife, **Danny Bernstein**, is an avid hiker who has written four books on the subject and hiked thousands of miles of trails all over the world.

Marty Gillen votes for the Oscars as a member of the Directors Guild. He spent his career producing TV commercials in New York City and won an Addy award for a Hollywood Bread ad.

Since "retiring" in Asheville, **Marty Gillen** has produced the annual Hard Lox Jewish Food and Heritage Festival and helped to choose movies for the Jewish Film Festival. He has been an active fundraiser and works tirelessly to help document Asheville's Jewish history. He conducted more than 50 interviews for the JCC's 75th anniversary, and these recordings will be housed as part of the JCC archives at the Pack Library North Carolina Collection.

Rising Stars

So much talent continues to come out of Asheville's Jewish community; and looking at our young adults, it is clear that the future is bright. These members of the next generation have gotten the support they needed from our "village" to grow and thrive:

While still in high school, **Elizabeth Gergel** performed Kol Nidre on the cello at CBHT. Elizabeth was awarded a prestigious McNair Scholarship to attend the University of South Carolina, where she received her undergraduate degree. Today, she is pursuing a master's degree in Cello Performance at the University of Oregon.

Noah Ratner literally grew up at CBHT, where his father, Rabbi Robert Ratner, was the beloved spiritual leader for many years. In this nurturing atmosphere, Noah was encouraged to follow his passion, and thus, honed his golf skills. He won two gold medals at the 2009 Maccabiah Games and helped the American team to a five-stroke win over Israel in the team competition. Since then, he has won numerous awards for his talents and is now a professional golfer.

The younger generation is continuing the tradition of healing the world and creating community. **Charlotte Grant** was a Peace Corp Volunteer in Tanzania and **Caleb Rudow** served in Zambia (and continued for a third year with US Aid to Developing Countries). **Josh Rudow** served in Ecuador with World Teach, which places recent college graduates in high schools and community colleges around the world. **Julie Goodstadt Josipovich** is the Senior Director of Development Operations with Moishe House in Charlotte; Moishe House provides a vibrant Jewish community for young adults by supporting young leaders as they create meaningful home-based Jewish experiences for themselves and their peers. This generation is an important link in the continuous chain of Jewish heritage and traditions.

Preserving Our History

The long history of Asheville's Jewish community's efforts to maintain its heritage while contributing to its hometown is the foundation upon which the thriving present-day Jewish institutions are built. Many of the people mentioned here are continuing their family traditions. There is a thread of similar talent or a connection to an ancestor that enabled that person to excel. We are very fortunate to have many of these stories, photographs and mementos preserved in the Jewish Life in Western North Carolina collection at the University of North Carolina-Asheville's Ramsey Library, Special Collections and at the Pack Memorial Library, North Carolina Collection that houses the JCC's and various family and business archives. Both can be accessed through the internet or by visiting these locations.

Additions to these collections are always welcomed. Consider a family collection at either archive if you have photographs or ephemera related to Asheville history. Items are filed, scanned and put in a safe environment in acid free folders. They become treasured sources to learn about the past and are accessible to all.

Shirley Cohen

Asheville Living Treasures

Asheville Living Treasures was started in 2010 to honor the elders of Asheville and Buncombe County who have greatly contributed to making our community a better place to live. These outstanding honorees are publically recognized and their stories are recorded for future generations. Jewish community members **Hyman Dave** (See photo on page 74), **Shirley Cohen** and **Charls Bolno** have all received this award.

Charls Bolno

The Jewish community always believed and adhered to supporting each other in business, but social discrimination made it a necessity. Being excluded from local country clubs or civic organizations closed economic doors, as these clubs were where business people cut deals, where the insurance agent met the banker, the realtor or the developer. Not being included in this economy, Jewish community members turned inward. Their families and the larger Jewish community assisted Jewish professionals and business people financially and as clients or customers. Asheville city directories record multiple examples of family members working in their own business or for another member of the Jewish community. Joseph Dave worked for Siegfried Sternberg; Jack Doloboff moved from New York to work for Rudolf Gumpert; Karl Straus came to work for his uncle Harry Straus.

Jan Schochet and Sharon Fahrer, as History@Hand, documented over 435 of the Jewish retail businesses in their project, *The Family Store, A History of the Jewish Businesses of Downtown Asheville, 1880-1990.* This exhibit can be seen virtually in the UNC Asheville D. Hiden Ramsey Special Collections. Following is a snapshot of Asheville's non-retail Jewish businesses, engaged in manufacturing, wholesale distribution and restaurants.

Manufacturing

Textiles

The opening of mills kept Jews on the move from one location to another, nationwide and locally. As new immigrants followed the rail lines, so they also followed the factories. Booms and busts increased and decreased the Jewish population. Jews were not generally factory workers, but rather industrialists, labor organizers, accountants and managers, or shopkeepers whose customers were laborers, observed historian Leonard Rogoff.

Cone Mills

The Asheville Cotton Mill (Courtesy of the North Carolina Collection, Pack Library)

The story of Cone Mills is a classic American "rags to riches" tale. Herman Kahn, a German Jew who immigrated to America in 1846, became a peddler of dry goods, leather, soaps and perfume. He eventually opened a store and later a wholesale grocery business; and in this endeavor moving to merchandising and distribution. He also changed the family name to Cone. Two of Herman's twelve children, Moses and Ceasar, went into the wholesale grocery business, and in this endeavor, they dealt with textile mills and company stores, enabling them to become familiar with industrial marketing styles. By the 1880s, the family began to invest in southern mills. In the late 1880s, Moses became the president of the C.E. Graham Manufacturing Company in Asheville. Graham had been a customer of H. Cone and Sons and apparently felt they could help finance his plant. The Cones thought investment in Asheville would be lucrative, as the city had finally gotten rail service and was growing rapidly, providing a source of cheap labor. The Cone brothers went on to amass one of the South's largest textile empires. Their most popular fabrics were denim and soft flannel which they were the first to brand.

Frederick W. Cone: 1905-1910 President of CBHT. (Courtesy of Ramsey Library Special Collections)

As their empire expanded, Moses and Ceasar brought relatives into their business operations to supply capital, skills and moral support. Their brother Frederick managed the Asheville Cotton Mill. In 1889, Moses purchased a house for his sister Carrie (1861-1927) and her husband Moses D. Long (1853-1936) on Park Avenue, adjacent to the property of C.E. Graham and a short distance from the Cone's Asheville Cotton Mill. M.D. Long was one of the 27 charter members of CBHT. The 1904-05 Asheville City directory lists Fred boarding at the Battery Park Hotel.

Inspired by the Biltmore Estate, Moses Cone built a mansion in the Blue Ridge Mountains (now a craft center on the Blue Ridge Parkway). Its colonial revival style of architecture portrayed an image of Anglo Saxon Protestantism. The house served to distance him from his old world immigrant and religious roots and assimilate him into American society. (Courtesy of Sharon Fahrer).

The Asheville Cotton Mill, part of the Cone Mills Corporation (later named Prosperity Mills), closed in 1953, after efforts failed to modernize it. The mill stood empty for 40 years until RiverLink and the Preservation Society of Asheville and Buncombe County redeveloped it as artists' studios. Most of the mill burned on April 2, 1995, but a remaining portion of the mill still stands in Asheville's River Arts District.

Vanderbilt Shirt Company, Inc.

The Vanderbilt Shirt Company had no connection to the family who built the Biltmore House. As Mrs. Watts, a former employee put it, people in Asheville just liked to name things for Biltmore and the Vanderbilts. (Courtesy of Ramsey Library Special Collections)

Milton Lurey, Herman Silver and Herbert Wadopian started the Vanderbilt Shirt Company. They manufactured men's dress shirts, but before long, they were doing contract work for other companies. One of their big clients was Levi Strauss, for whom they made western style shirts and later women's shirts. They also produced shirts and jackets for the US military. Their original factory was located in downtown Asheville, first in Tingle Alley and later on the corner of Walnut Street and Lexington Avenue. (Its sign is still hanging over the entrance on Walnut Street.) Milton and Herbert had previously owned United Tire Retreading Company, but thought manufacturing shirts would be a cleaner business.

The partners were forward-thinking employers. When they noticed that several of their employees were missing front teeth, they invited a health department nurse to speak to them about nutrition. After a fire damaged much of the building in the late 1960s, they built a new factory on the outskirts of Asheville, which included an outlet shop and daycare center. It is not surprising that some of the employees worked for the company for 30 or more years. In 1971, the owners won North Carolina's "Employer of the Year" Award in the "Over 200 Employees" category.

As American companies began to outsource the manufacturing process, the Vanderbilt Shirt Company turned to Haiti. This led to the ultimate undoing of the company. During the political unrest of the late 1980s following the ouster of the Duvalier regime, the Vanderbilt factory in Port-au-Prince was destroyed along with all the machinery and inventory. The company never recovered from this loss. They operated in a smaller facility on Asheville's French Broad Avenue until the early 1990s, when they closed their doors for good.

Hadley Cashmere

Hadley Cashmere, located in Weaverville, was one of the leading manufacturers of camel hair, cashmere and vicuna sweaters in the United States from the 1940s through the 1970s. It was owned by Richard (Dick) on the right, and Jane Haber. (Courtesy of Ramsey Library Special Collections)

Audie Bayer remembers: "In 1955, when I went to Cornell, they (the Habers) invited my mother and me to their factory, and I got to pick out lots and lots of cashmeres to take to the COLD North. They sold them to us at cost. I arrived at Cornell, met Bobby (her future husband) the second week, and shared my cashmeres with my whole freshman dorm. I had so many!"

Besides cashmere sweaters, Hadley also made coordinated wool skirts and silk blouses. These matched sets were very popular with college girls in the 1950s and early 1960s. The Habers' son John (one of three children) started Tanglewood Children's Theater, a part of the Asheville Community Theater, when he was twelve years old. This launched him into a career in the theater first in Chapel Hill and later in New York City.

.

Biltmore Industries

Biltmore Industries was established as a craft school to teach marketable skills to the youth of Appalachia. Its forty looms produced homespun fabric worn by the rich and famous, including American presidents Coolidge, Hoover, and Franklin Roosevelt and their wives. (Courtesy of Pack library).

Harry Blomberg (1904-1991) had wheels in his head because he loved automobiles. A native Ashevillian, he owned several motor inns in downtown Asheville for people to park rag top cars indoors as well as a service station and a Cadillac La Salle car dealership. (Courtesy of Ramsey Library Special Collections)

In 1954, Harry Blomberg purchased Biltmore Industries. Demand for its homespun fabrics was dwindling in the face of a rapidly automating textile industry, and the business and the buildings were deteriorating. Oral history tells us that Harry went to Biltmore Industries to buy a still, previously used for making moonshine, as a "conversation piece" for his Lake Lure house. When he inquired as to the price, he was told that the still belonged to Mr. Fred Seely and the United States government and could not be sold; however, he could buy Biltmore Industries. So, he did. Harry restarted production of Biltmore's homespun fabrics, keeping the operation going for an additional 25 years. In 1980, Biltmore Industries finally closed, but the property remained in the family. Barbara Blomberg, her sister Marilyn and Marilyn's husband, S.M. (Buddy) Patton, renovated and restored the original six, English-style cottages and grounds. In 1992, they opened the Grovewood Gallery, which included craft studios for local artisans. A small museum of the history of Biltmore Industries and the Estes Winn Car Museum, which houses Harry's antique car collection and the still, are also located on the grounds.

Highland and Goldbloom Manufacturing

Stan Golden (1923-2008) grew up in the time of the indefatigable American spirit. He believed that if something did not work, you kept trying until you found what did work. When the war came, you served your country. You worked hard and provided for your family. This was Stan's American life. (Courtesy of Betty Pollock Golden)

Stan Golden was a gentle giant (his nickname). He was a soft-spoken man of few words, but when he spoke, you wanted to remember what he said. In addition, he had a terrific memory. He was born in St. Paul, Minnesota, where his father, Harold Goldbloom was a salesperson for Hart Schaffner and Marx men's clothing. When the Great Depression hit, Mr. Goldbloom (the original family name) took traveling sales positions. The family traveled with him, and whenever it came time to give up the territory he was working in or sell another type of merchandise, they moved. Stan's father worked his way across the country, from St. Paul to Los Angeles, selling Moto Sway machines to gas stations. The Moto was a lift that rocked cars up in the air so that their springs could be greased. During this time, the family moved every three or four months from one end of the country to the other. When they moved back to Cleveland, Stan's father started a siding business with his two brothers-in-law. This is what he continued to do when the family came to Asheville in 1940. By then, Stan was a junior in high school and had moved twenty-one times. The constant moving made the Goldbloom family very

close. After Stan graduated from Lee Edwards High School (now Asheville High), he went to Georgia Tech to study architecture, decided he did not like that and transferred to North Carolina State University to study textile management. While there, he joined the Enlisted Reserve Corps (ERC) thinking he would be able to finish school. Just Stan's luck, even the ERC was called into active duty. On the move again, he started training in Macon, Georgia, was sent to five US locations and overseas to France, Belgium, Germany and the Philippines before being discharged. Back in Asheville, he married the love of his life, Betty Pollock. Betty recalls they moved nine times in the first year of their marriage! Moreover, Stan remembered every place he lived growing up, as well as where he was sent during World War II.

After their marriage, Stan worked in Betty's father's shoe store, Pollock's, and later for his own father, who now owned a suit, coat and dress business called Highland Manufacturing on Coxe Avenue. The factory was in the "contracting" business. This meant that a company would ship their material to Highland, which would do the cutting and the sewing, and then send the finished garments back to the contractor. Around 1953, Harold set up a showroom at the factory to sell directly to the public at wholesale prices. Originally, called Highland, the name was later changed to Goldbloom, Inc.

Harold Goldbloom, Stan Golden's father, served as President of CBHT 1947-1948 (d. 1956). (Courtesy of Ramsey Library Special Collections)

Stan and Betty's fathers bought them a dress shop on Patton Avenue. Stan would drop Betty at the store, and then go to the factory. At noon, he would come back to run the store while Betty taught school. Then it was back to the the factory and back to the store to close it for the day. Despite his long workdays, Stan was active in CBHT and other religious organizations.

Blue Jay Knitting Mills

Julius Blum was a Holocaust survivor who came to the United States after World War II. With the aid of a scholarship from the Hebrew Immigrant Aid Society (HIAS), he studied textile engineering

Julius Blum's (1925-2003) passion was teaching Jewish studies. He spoke about his life in Czechoslovakia before the war and his experiences in the Holocaust. He established a fund at UNC Asheville to offer classes on Jewish studies and to support programs sponsored by the CJS. (Courtesy of Ramsey Library Special Collection)

at Georgia Tech. Julius began his career working for U.S. Rubber Company in the tire cord division in South Carolina and was later transferred to New York City. He then took a position with Butte Knitting Mills, a division of Jonathan Logan, in Spartanburg, South Carolina. In 1966, Julius moved his family to Asheville and started his own company on Haywood Street in a garage rented from Harry Blomberg. This became Blue Jay Mills, which Julius eventually sold to Avondale Mills from Alabama. Julius then started another company, Merit Knitting Mills. Both companies produced double knit fabric used by clothing manufacturers. Merit was employing 150 to 200 people into the 1990s, when it closed as manufacturing moved overseas.

Connie Fashions Manufacturing, Inc.

Lily Gluck Lerner grew up on a middle-class farm in rural Hungary. At age sixteen, she and her family were rounded up for deportation to Auschwitz concentration camp. Lily, her sister and cousin were lined up at a rail station in Budapest with thousands of other young Jewish women. Heinrich Himmler and Adolf Eichmann happened to be presiding over this particular deportation. Himmler glanced at the roster and noticed that the three girls were family.

He ordered them to disperse into separate lines. They obeyed the command; however, the moment that the Germans were distracted, they jumped back in the same line despite the risk of being shot for not following orders. Because the girls had each other, they survived Auschwitz. Near the end of the war, they were part of a small group of surviving teenage girls transferred to a munitions factory in Germany. The owner of the factory treated the girls well, and they all survived. Lily's memoir, *The Silence*, documents these experiences.

Harry Lerner (1923-1999) grew up in a small Hungarian town, the son of shopkeepers of modest means. At the start of World War II, he was drafted into the Hungarian army. However, midway through the war, when the Nazis took control over Hungary, they ordered the removal of all Jews from the military. Jewish enlisted men were told that they had been relieved from duty and were to report to the Russian front. They believed that they were being sent to build roads. Suspicious, Harry escaped from a road detail and joined a group of partisans. Several days later, the Jews in Harry's detail were executed. At the end of the war, Harry, again distrusting the situation, escaped the Russian liberators, and fled over the Alps to American troops. The Russians murdered all Jewish partisans who stayed.

Harry and Lily Lerner moved to Asheville in the early 1960s and started Connie Fashions Manufacturing, Inc., which included a clothing factory and three retail outlets. Their "Traveler by Connie" label produced women's clothing, including blouses, pants, suits, slacks, dresses and shirts. The Lerner's new lives were prosperous and filled with love and a wonderful family. Their oldest daughter, Connie, became a Miss North Carolina. A gazebo near the parking lot of the Beaver Lake Bird Sanctuary bears a plaque in memory of Lily Lerner.

Mars Manufacturing

Morry Bard studied textile dyeing at Lowell Tech (now University of Massachusetts Lowell). After graduation, he opened a dye facility for hosiery in New York. This expanded into knit fabric, and he set up his first finishing plant in Union, South Carolina. Around 1945, the company moved to Asheville, where they made full-fashion women's hosiery with the seams in the back. Later they manufactured seamless hosiery, becoming one of the first manufacturers of panty hose in the United States. Mars was also one of the first manufacturers of children's and women's stretch tights. In the early 1960s, they also produced men's tights, some of which were worn by the New York Giants football team.

Robert (Bob) Bayer, who married Morry's daughter, Audrey (Audie), phased out the hosiery operation and pioneered the introduction of disposable

Mars (the initials of the Bards: Morry, Audrey, Ron and Sallie) Hosiery Mill was a small family-owned manufacturing company operated by Morry Bard. The water tower was part of the operation to meet insurance compliance. They manufactured 2.4 million pairs of stockings per year. Two to Three hundred people worked in the factory, which operated 24 hours a day (Courtesy of Ramsey Library Special Collections)

retail apparel in the 1960s and 1970s. The name of the company was changed from Mars Hosiery Manufacturing to Mars Manufacturing.

About 1961, Bob saw a sample of nonwoven fabric and immediately envisioned utilizing it for

disposable undershorts for the Army in VietNam. Unfortunately, testing found the undershorts caused chaffing of the legs, so the product was never manufactured. However, the process proved applicable in other ways.

Mars developed a "paper" dress. This seemed destined to fail until paper manufacturers Scott and Kimberly-Stevens used a paper dress as a marketing tool to promote their other products. With Scott's nationwide advertising paving the way for acceptance, Mars immediately went into production. Ron Bard became the New York sales representative and Audie developed a full line of clothing under the "Wastebasket Boutique" label that included foil evening gowns, bathing suits, paper children's clothes, men's vests, shirts, pants, football jerseys and apparel items for major corporations, political campaigns, even paper hostess' ensembles with matching napkins and placemats and paint-it-yourself designs. The dresses averaged four or five wearings.

To promote Mars' plain white dress that came with a watercolor paint set, Andy Warhol adorned one at a "happening." He stenciled "fragile" onto the dress and signed it "Dali." The garment was donated to the Brooklyn Museum of Art. Ron Bard appeared on the *Today Show* with Barbara Walters and the quiz show *To Tell The Truth* where he stumped the panel.

By the late 1960s, the fashion line lost its popularity. Mars immediately turned its attention to what was

The August 11, 1966 issue of Woman's Wear Daily ran an article that said:

"Mars Manufacturing Company wrote a new chapter in the apparel industry book when it unleashed the $1.29 throwaway paper shift. Now the red hot firm is pressing plans for an epic fashion expansion."

viewed as another huge potential market: disposable work clothing, including lab coats, coveralls, aprons, shoe covers and caps. In 1970, the Bayer family sold Mars Manufacturing to Work Wear Corporation and formed another company, American Threshold, which focused on the production of paper hospital and laboratory goods. Bob retired when they sold that company in 1998.

There were other Jewish manufacturers as well. In 1940, **Philip Michalove** owned Carolina Rayon Products Company, Inc. producing underwear at 80 ½ Patton Avenue. **Joseph Greenberg** ran Kar Lyn Corporation, manufacturing boys shirts; and **Ira Rosenstock** of Glendale Manufacturing Corporation made women's lingerie. In the 1960s, **Edward Feld** (father of Robin Jane Feld) owned Artex Manufacturing Company, manufacturing rugs from textile scraps.

Rags to Riches

The rag business refers to collecting pieces of cloth like textile waste and repurposing it by washing and sanitizing or reworking it into a useable form such as thread. The disposable wiper business evolved from the rag business.

Sanitary Wiper Company

Phillip and Irving Ness came to Asheville in the 1930s. The Ness brothers owned the Asheville Junk Company and ran the Sanitary Wiper Company, which manufactured wiping cloths and paper, tissue and cleaning products for all segments of industry. Later, Phillip Ness owned Ness Disposables and Philip Ness Manufacturing. He sold his company to Sam Slosman, his brother-in-law, in 1946.

The Slosman Corporation

Bernard Slosman founded the Slosman Corporation as a rag business in Pittsfield, Massachusetts in 1902. His son, Samuel Slosman, focused on traditional textile products, manufacturing dust and polishing cloths and rags from cotton and wool remnants.

Nettie and Samuel (Sam) Slosman. Sam moved the Slosman Corporation to Asheville in 1935. (Courtesy of Sandy Slosman)

As fibers changed in the textile industry, Benson Slosman, one of Sam's sons, started a synthetic fiber division using nylon and polyester waste. Samuel's younger son, Fred, began as a territory sales representative, working while he completed his last two years at North Carolina State University, where he received a bachelor's degree in textiles in 1961. Benson eventually moved into commercial real estate development; but Fred remained in the Slosman Corporation, which eventually manufactured disposable wiping rags.

Both Benson and Fred, were involved in the Asheville Jewish and civic community. Both served as President of CBI. Fred was also president of the JCC, a member of Sigma Alpha Mu at North Carolina State University for fifty years, a 32nd degree Mason, serving on the boards of First Commercial Bank and the March of Dimes, and belonged to Chaine des Rotisseurs (a fine dining organization).

Jeff Slosman was named Carolina Small Business Person of the Year for 2015 by the U.S. Small Business Administration (SBA). (Courtesy of Ellen Knoefel)

Fourth generation Jeff Slosman, Fred's son, started his own manufacturing business in 1996. National Wiper Alliance (NWA) manufactures industrial wipes and cloths, recycling nonwoven materials and converting them into dry wiping products. From washcloths to heavy duty cleaning cloths, NWA supplies reusable and disposable wipes to various industries in the manufacturing, food service, healthcare, government and other sectors with specialized needs. Their niche is custom printing on their products.

Broad River Processing Company

Theodore and Rebecca Kahn brought their family to Asheville from South Carolina in the 1920s. They opened a dry goods store in West Asheville and lived in that area of the city. Their son, Mortimer (Mort) Kahn, Sr. (1906-1986), managed their store, then called The Bon Ton, in 1930. In 1941, Mort was president of Sternberg and Company and his wife, Adela, was vice president. In the late 1940s, Mort bought the J.A. Baker Packing Company ("Home of All Pig," their advertisement boasted) and expanded it to become the Kahn Company, Inc. and the Broad River Processing Company. The companies dyed and finished wiping cloth for the furniture industry and exported textiles. They were also in the hide business, brokering carloads of hides for shoes, boots and kid gloves. Mort's son Fred, recalls that working with hides was tough and smelly, but to his family it was the smell of dollars.

Because Mort Sr. was forced to give up plans to become a physician after his parents died, and he had to support his two younger sisters, he established the Mortimer Kahn Management scholarship at UNC Asheville to provide financial aid to students majoring in business. As a man of great integrity, he believed in treating everyone fairly and working hard.

The Dave Steel Company location is now part of the River Arts District. (Courtesy of Dave Steel)

Steel Fabrication

Dave Steel Company

Yosel Teivo, born in Lithuania, came to America as a child in 1907. Here he took the name Joseph Dave. Joseph's father, Philip Dave, had already settled in Durham, North Carolina when he sent for his wife, daughter and son. Joseph went on to college and graduated with an engineering degree from the University of Cincinnati. In 1923, he landed in Asheville for a sales job at Southern Steel & Cement Company, owned by Don Elias. Once hired, he asked to do something unconventional for someone with a college degree: he dressed in overalls and worked with the laborers in the warehouse and on the trucks. Within six months, Joseph went to work for Siegfried Sternberg who, in addition to dealing

At first, the Dave Steel Company had a single warehouse with all fabrication being done in an open lot without any heavy equipment. (Courtesy of Dave Steel)

in junk and hides, had started a small steel business for which he needed a manager. Sternberg later purchased Southern Steel & Cement Company.

By 1929, Joseph was confident enough to found the Dave Steel Company, furnishing structural steel for small bridgework and local businesses construction projects. The company grew along with Western North Carolina, its first major project being the American Enka plant in 1932, which later became BASF. Joseph's brother Hyman joined the company in 1934, after receiving a degree in Civil Engineering from North Carolina State University.

With the onset of World War II, the steel plant was retooled to manufacture parts for the construction of LSMs (Landing Ship Medium) that were used

For its work during the war years, the company received the Army-Navy "E" award in both 1944 and 1945. (Courtesy of Dave Steel)

to land troops on beaches. After the war, Dave Steel returned to supplying structural steel for the industrial and commercial construction market, expanding operations into Ohio and later Chesnee, South Carolina.

Joseph Dave (1897-1983) was active in Asheville civic organizations, becoming the first Jewish president of the Asheville Lions Club in 1932. (Courtesy of Dave Steel)

Judaism was very important to Joseph. He joined CBHT in 1923. As soon as members learned that he could sing, he was immediately invited to join the temple choir. Joseph felt that the most important thing he did for the temple was to help in the construction of the new house of worship and religious school buildings. Rabbi Sidney Unger, spiritual leader of CBHT at the time, took the position in Asheville, in part, because he and Dave were friends from Cincinnati.

Hyman Dave became president of Dave Steel in 1950 when his brother, Joseph, moved to Cincinnati to open a new plant. He was also active in CBHT, which he joined in 1935, serving as president twice and head of the cemetery committee for 45 years. Hyman joined Kiwanis in 1939 and had perfect attendance for 66 of his 75-year membership. When his grandson, Jeff Slosman, started NWA in the mid-1990s, Hyman worked with him. Hyman lived an active life until he passed away in 2011, at over 100 years of age. On his 100th birthday, he said, "I've had a wonderful life in 100 years. I don't regret a day of it."

Hyman Dave (1910-2011) retired from Dave Steel in 1976, after 40 years, only to begin a new career in food service as the manager of the Asheville Downtown City Club (1979-1986) and the Asheville Country Club. The City Club called him back again in 1994. Hyman retired three times in all. (Courtesy of Ramsey Library Special Collections)

Dave Steel was the last big manufacturing facility operating in Asheville's River Arts District. In 2010, they closed their original location at the corner of Roberts Street and Clingman Avenue; as the area gentrified, it was no longer practical to operate from there. Their facilities remain on Meadow Road in Asheville, and in Chesnee, South Carolina. The leadership of Dave Steel in Asheville has passed in succession to Joseph's son, Jerome (Jerry), then to Jerry's son, Jeff, the third generation to run Dave Steel.

Junk Dealers

Though Jews were not lawfully restricted from engaging in any professions in America as they had been in Europe, immigrants often went into businesses they were familiar with from the old country. Dealing in junk (trading and acting as middlemen) was one of these familiar professions. It served as a way to make nothing into something, and linked the rural economy with urban markets.

The 1937 Asheville City Directory lists four junk dealers and they were all Jewish:

- S. Sternberg and Company, Siegfried Sternberg, 353 Depot Road;

- Asheville Junk and Hide Company, Philip and Irving Ness, 306 Patton Avenue;

- Consolidated Hide and Metal, Joseph Sternberg, 155 Roberts Street; and

- Frank Silverman Company, Frank Silverman, Swannanoa Road.

S. Sternberg and Company

Siegfried Sternberg, a cattle-trader from Aurich, Germany, immigrated to Asheville (via Galveston, Texas) in 1900. Here he operated a tannery, buying

Siegfried Sternberg, (1865-1939) President of CBHT: 1917-1920, 1925-1927, 1928-1929 (Courtesy of Ramsey Library Special Collections),

cowhides which were by-products of the regional meat industry, and processing them into shoe leather. Sternberg also recycled metal and furs. His motto was "We buy anything and we sell everything." Siegfried was in partnership with his brother-in-law, Gustav Lichtenfels who had also come from Germany. (Gustav married Edna Long, daughter of Moses Long.)

Consolidated Hide and Metal

Siegfried's son, Joseph, continued in the same line of work, operating Consolidated Hide and Metal. He would create jackets from scraps of shoe leather; and later, when leather went to the war effort, he fashioned Snoopy-style aviator helmets out of scrap rubber from the Dayton Rubber Company in Asheville, which made rafts. Even kitchen grease collected from regional military camps was trucked to Consolidated to be rendered useful again. Consolidated also purchased scrap metal, which consisted of about

Joseph Sternberg (1907-1968) President CBHT 1942-1945 (Courtesy of Ramsey Library Special Collection)

fifty grades of brass and twenty-five of aluminum. This required people to meticulously evaluate the odds and ends and sort them. For this, Joe hired African-American women he knew from the textile waste industry, promoting some to supervisory positions. Joe was in business with Alfred Lichtenfels.

Conservco

Jerry Sternberg "grew up" on Depot Street, working alongside his father's employees and observing the "technique" of deal making. Jerry was in the waste-hauling business, as well as junk, and later became a real estate developer.

Jack Doloboff came to Asheville in 1957 to work for Rudolf Gumpert, who was in the textile waste business. He was referred for the job by his wife Arlene's uncle, Charles Parmet who was the director of the JCC at the time. Jack later went into the trash and scrap business with Jerry Sternberg which lasted 40 years. They sold their company, Conservco, a trash hauler, to Waste Management. Jack and his wife Arlene were instrumental in bringing The Chabad House to Asheville.

Shulimson Brothers

The Shulimson siblings in front of their business located in Asheville's River District. Pictured left to right Eadie, Morrie, Mary Shulimson Tabashneck, Bill and Ben Shulimson. (Courtesy of the Shulimson family)

Brothers William (Bill), Morris (Morrie), and Ben Shulimson purchased Harrison Auto Parts from Phillip Ness in 1953 and added a scrap and recycling component which they operated as Shulimson Brothers Company, Inc. In the early 1960s, they sold the auto parts business and reopened just a parts and scrap business. The brothers were philanthropic and active in the community. Bill started an essay contest for high school students on "What did America mean to me?" He was awarded the key to the city from both Asheville and Olean, N.Y. (where he lived prior to moving to Asheville) for his civic contributions. Morrie was an avid supporter of the arts, helping finance John Cram, art gallery pioneer, in his first business. Ben, besides fundraising within the Jewish community, was a Shriner and early supporter of Meals on Wheels and Asheville Community Theatre.

The business closed in 1996 because the Norfolk Southern Railroad (which owned the property) would not renew the lease.

The Frank Silverman Company

Frank Silverman (1891-1942) appeared in the 1927 City Directory as a dealer of used auto parts. Frank

The Frank Silverman Company on Swannanoa River Road dealt in junk, auto parts and conduit piping over the years. (Courtesy of Sharon Fahrer)

is the person who gave an initial donation for a JCC so that his son would have a place to socialize with other Jewish youth. Jerome (Jerry) Silverman was an employee in his business, but later established his own junk business.

Textile Waste

Textile waste is created from the manufacturing process and through consumer use; it could include irregular garments and hosiery. Textile processors, brokers and handlers grade the scraps, bail them and ship them to end-users domestically or, more often, to other countries. There, waste is ground up to use as stuffing for mattresses or to be remade into yarn. Cotton material is used for stuffing and paper manufacturing.

Isaac Gradman Company

Isaac Gradman had been selling used batteries for his father's company in Louisville, Kentucky during the Great Depression, when he met Phillip Ness at a gas station in North Carolina. They talked for a while, and Ness offered

Isaac Gradman (1906-1963), as President of CBHT 1945-1947. He also served as the President of the Fifth District of B'nai B'rith. (Courtesy of Ramsey Library Special Collections)

Isaac a job as a truck driver for his new company in Asheville. Isaac accepted and moved his family to Asheville. He eventually left the Ness company and started the Isaac Gradman Company, which recycled wool, nylon, lace and hosiery waste. Harriette Winner recalls that she loved to go with her father, Isaac, to watch workers cut up fabric at long tables and load big bales onto railroad cars right outside the warehouse near the French Broad River. The Isaac Gradman Company became one of the biggest hosiery waste dealers in the United States sending material to Europe and Asia, according to Barney Gradman, Isaac's son. As more modern and efficient machinery came into use, the textile waste business dwindled.

Harriette also remembers that on trips to Kentucky to visit family, they always stopped in Corbin to eat fried chicken at Colonel Sander's restaurant. The Colonel would be seated at a table for two, dressed in his white suit. As they left the restaurant, he would ask her father if the children ate well. The answer was always "yes," so he would give her and Barney a tootsie pop. Barney was at one time considered one of the best Jewish athletes in North Carolina, excelling in fast pitch softball, basketball and football.

The Asheville of the manufacturing era is a fading memory. Though some of the buildings still exist, their original occupants may be long forgotten. The industries along the rivers, plagued periodically by floods, started going out of business in the 1940s. Junk yards made good use of the blighted area. Textiles closed or left later between the 1970s and 1990s.

A few businesses, like Dave Steel and NWA, continue to be run by family members. Some families have changed their businesses in their locations, as Biltmore Industries became the Grovewood. Some descendants remain: Slosmans,

Shulimsons, Blombergs, Sternbergs, Bayers, Winners and Kahns. Their forbearers created an economy and were part of the diverse fabric of Asheville. They were honest and hardworking, creating something from nothing to make a better life in America.

Wholesale / Retail

Middlemount Gardens

Charles Webb, President of the Citizen Company (newspaper), brought Otto Buseck, a horticulturist, from New York, to manage a wholesale flower growing business on his estate, Middlemount, located on Sulphur Springs Road in West Asheville. It was quite successful, becoming the largest carnation grower in the southeast. The enterprise provided all the flowers for Cornelia Vanderbilt's wedding in 1924. Otto also designed the gravesites in Riverside Cemetery for 18 German merchant marines who died in an influenza epidemic while they were interred in Hot Springs during World War I. Their remains were moved to Riverside in the 1930s.

Max Crohn, Sr. moved to Asheville for his health from Memphis, Tennessee in 1919. His uncle Otto taught him the florist and horticulture business that he eventually took over. Middlemount opened a retail florist shop on Haywood Street in the 1920s. They sold the greenhouses in 1949 or 1950 and the retail store in 1975.

Max Crohn, Sr. was one of a handful of Jews who joined the Asheville Country Club during the Depression when the club needed money and so eased the restrictions on Jewish membership. He also served as president of CBHT 1940-1942. (Courtesy of Ramsey Library Special Collections).

Asheville Showcase and Fixture Company

Walking north on Broadway, it is easy to miss "Mr. Equip" painted on the wall beside the doorway to number 57. What, you might wonder, is he doing there? The sign is left from the time that this building was one of the locations of the Asheville Showcase and Fixture Company. Leon Rocamora, Sr. started the company as Asheville Candy Company in 1920. He sold wholesale candy, but customers began asking for refrigeration and display cases. Thus, it evolved into a wholesale restaurant supply business. Leon, Sr. emigrated from Hamburg, Germany in 1918 and moved to Asheville in 1920. He died suddenly from influenza in 1935. His wife, Fan, left with two teenage sons to support, jumped in to run her husband's business. Her son, Leon Rocamora, Jr., remembers when his father died. "I was in high school at that time, at Lee Edwards, and I would go and work all afternoon, to help my Mother out with the store."

Fan Rocamora (1891-1977) was the only woman in America who was active in the restaurant supply business for most of her career, which lasted into the late 1960s. (Courtesy of Ramsey Library Special Collections)

Prior to taking over the family business, Fan had a millinery shop. During the Great Depression, she also took in boarders, many of whom would return each summer because they enjoyed her cooking. Fan kept a jug of moonshine in the back of Asheville Showcase in case her customers were thirsty!

Asheville Showcase and Fixture Company on Broadway continued as a family business run by the Rocamora sons until, in their 80s, they sold it. (Courtesy of Ramsey Library Special Collections)

Galumbeck and Company

Galumbeck and Company was a hosiery wholesaler and jobber on Broadway in the 1940s owned by Tippi Galumbeck father of Phyllis Sultan. A jobber is similar to a wholesaler. They purchase product from company "A" and then sell the product to company "B"—usually within the same industry and not to consumers. Wholesalers typically buy from factories and then sell to retailers. Jobbers typically buy from other wholesalers (at discounted prices) and occasionally direct from factories. If a mill has excess fabric or a wholesaler has received a store return or a cancellation, they can contact a jobber to help liquidate the inventory.

Electric Supply Company of Asheville Inc. (ESCO)

Gene Winner went into the electrical, industrial and plumbing supply business, operating thirty-six stores. Gene attributed part of his business success to loyal employees. He offered them a profit-sharing plan and a retirement plan when it was not mandatory and treated them like family.

ESCO claimed that one of its stores had the longest sales counter east of the Continental Divide! (Courtesy of Gene Winner)

Gene Winner was the first Jewish baby to be born in the hospital in Sylva, North Carolina in 1933. Some local folks asked to see him to check if he had horns, a common belief among gentiles of the time. (This perception was due to a mistranslation in the *King James Bible* that said Moses had horns instead of light around his head.) Gene grew up in Morganton until his family moved to Asheville. His father and Harry Winner were brothers.

Morganton was a small town with few Jewish families. People within a 20-mile radius would gather to celebrate Jewish holidays and expose their children to Judaism. All the Jewish families were in retail. A circuit-riding Rabbi would come once a month to hold services. Their small group met in the chemistry building at Lenoir-Rhyne University. Once his family moved to Asheville in 1947, Gene became involved in BBYO and AZA, Jewish youth organizations.

Grocery Stores

Owning a neighborhood grocery store and sometimes living above or behind it was a way to start up the ladder to success, or at least make a living which enabled a family to send their children to college. The 1925, Asheville city directory lists at least eleven Jewish owned grocery stores, and the 1940 directory lists at least ten: Charles, Marcus and Samuel Book each had one, Simon Feldman, Harry Freeman, Morris Freeman, David Schandler, Lois Robins, Samuel Robins and Jake Rosen. In 1960, the Feldman's and the Schandlers still had their grocery stores.

Restaurants

D. Gross and Sons

In 1899, David Gross ran a fruit and confection stand on Pack Square. By 1918, Gross and Sons was operating as an "eating house." During the Great Depression, David was walking along Broadway and noticed a narrow alley between two three-story buildings. He opened an eatery in this space, which was only 40 inches wide and 85 feet long.

With the addition of a roof over the tables, the location became known as a "cafe." The restaurant specialized in hot dogs and ham sandwiches. A newspaper article noted that the establishment's main problem was trying to seat a fat customer at the far end of the counter. While a thin person could squeeze past other patrons, for a fat person to take a seat, all the other patrons had to be standing up to let him pass. By the time his sons, Charles and Leon, joined the business, the restaurant had moved to Pack Square.

David Gross (1865-1944) came to the United States from Budapest, Hungary in 1873. (Courtesy of Ramsey Library Special Collections)

Charles and Leon retired in 1945, and D. Gross and Sons closed.

Having more than a dozen children, Gross was described as the man with Asheville's biggest family and tiniest business. (Courtesy of Ramsey Library Special Collections)

The Old Heidelberg

Sitting prominently overlooking downtown Asheville from the east on Beaucatcher Mountain, is a large building, today known as Ardmion. Built in the 1890s, it was originally the Oliver Cromwell Hamilton Estate. The Great Depression took a toll on the Hamiltons; and in 1935, the estate was auctioned on the courthouse steps. Gus and Emma Adler, who owned The Old Heidelberg restaurant in East Asheville, purchased the property and re-opened in the Hamilton mansion.

Emma was "the hostess with the mostess" and Gus was the "genius in the kitchen," according to his stepson, John Hunter. (Courtesy of Ramsey Library Special Collections)

Old Heidelberg, named after Gus's home town in Germany, offered fine dining, dancing, spectacular views and great atmosphere. It served as a destination for many Jewish Ashevillians' social activities. When World War II broke out, the restaurant sign became a target for anti-German graffiti. Unfazed, in 1942 Gus and Emma renamed the restaurant The Sky Club in order to make it sound more American. Nothing else changed, and the Sky Club remained just as popular. It was Asheville's place to be seen.

The Adlers lived in Beau Castle, which was said to be the former estate stables converted to a residence near the former mansion. Gus died there in a fire in 1952. Though devastated, Emma kept the restaurant going.

Buncombe County did not allow sales of liquor by the glass in those days, so patrons of the Sky Club would bring their own bottles and pay a storage fee to keep them at the club. They would also be charged $1.00 for a bucket of ice and glasses when they wanted their drinks. However, on July 13, 1957, Emma was arrested (along with five other nightclub owners in Asheville) on charges of illegal resale of tax-paid liquor.

In the late 1940s and 1950s, film production came to Asheville. *Tap Roots*, *The Swan*, *The Great Locomotive Chase* and *Thunder Road* all had scenes filmed around the city and Emma catered all the on-location meals. The casts and crews often made the Sky Club their nighttime hangout. Fess Parker, Grace Kelly, Louis Jordan, Ward Bond, Susan Haywood and Robert Mitchum were among the luminaries who could be found there. Robert Mitchum even invited Emma to visit him in Hollywood, and she did! Charlton Heston, known as "Chuck," also frequented the club in the late 1940s, when he and his wife Lydia directed the Asheville Community Theater before moving on to Hollywood.

The Adlers tried several times to sell the Sky Club, but no one could keep up the quality and reputation of the establishment. Finally, in 1975, Emma sold the property; and it later was renovated into condominiums. The glamour of the Sky Club was lost, but the property still makes a grand impression overlooking downtown.

Vick's Restaurant

For a brief period in the late 1930s and early 1940s, Victor and Alex Avzradel and Morris Tarica, Sephardic Jews, ran Vick's Restaurant on Haywood Street and Vick's Grill on Pack Square.

McDonald's Franchises

Whitlock (Whit) Lees, a member of the Lipinsky family and descendent of Solomon Lipinsky (who founded Asheville's Bon Marché Department store), opened Asheville's first McDonald's on Tunnel Road around 1960. Leon Rocamora remembers telling Whit he would never make money selling fifteen-cent hamburgers and only making one-and-a-half cents on each. Whitlock went on to own several McDonald's franchises and left his wife a wealthy widow.

Schandler's Pickle Barrel

Schandler's Pickle Barrel was Asheville's definition of a Jewish delicatessen. Located at 50 Broadway in a former Pure Oil gas station, it served corned beef on rye, pastrami, and juicy wursts with sauerkraut and tangy potato salad. Run by Aaron Schandler, loyal staff served its customers for years. The building also housed Aaron's wife's hobbicraft business.

Aaron was the son of David, who moved his family to Asheville in the early 1900s. At first, the family made a living hemming handkerchiefs, and then David opened a cigar store. In the 1920s, David operated Schandler's Oak Street Cash Market, a grocery located next to the First Baptist Church on Oak Street; the family lived above the store. Urban renewal forced that business to close.

More Jewish-owned Restaurants

More Jewish restaurateurs have followed, serving delicious food: Kathy Shastri of the Windmill, Alan Laibson of the Savoy, Glenn and Gerry Goldberg of Goldberg's Deli, Mitchell Adler of Café on the Square, Eric Scheffer of Vinnie's, Jacob Sessoms of Table, Teri and Greg Siegel of Avenue M, Richard Laibson of Trevi and McGuffy's, Harry Goldberg of Harry's Bagels, and Sherrye Coggiola of The Cantina to mention a few. They have contributed to Asheville's "foodie destination" status. Is it coincidence that there are so many Jews involved in the restaurant industry when so much Jewish tradition revolves around food?

The orginal Schandler's Pickle Barrel sign hangs inside the Mellow Mushroom restaurant which now occupies the building. (Courtesy of Sharon Fahrer)

A Few More Businesses

Lesser-known businesses were owned by Jack Feingold, who owned Carolina Surplus Company, Al Goodman, who had a heavy equipment rental company, and Nemiah Goldstein, of Blue Ridge Trucking Company.

Today's Jewish business owners include the Kort and Kirsch families of Blossom's at Biltmore Park and the Baggie Goose, Devorah and Philip Holan of Payment Collect, Ted and Sherrill Zoller of Outdoor Bird Company, and Josh and Jane Tager of Natural Nosh. The Asheville Jewish Business Forum boasts numerous members, all of whom are listed on the AJBF's website

The diversity of the contributions of the entrepreneurs highlighted in this chapter reflects the development of Asheville's economic history and the adaptability and fluidity of its Jewish community. Their industriousness and business successes melded with the growth and character of Asheville, creating a strong collaborative community where the success of one contributes to the success of all.

The Asheville Jewish community is vibrant and growing with many opportunities for residents to connect to Judaism. No matter what the link, everyone is a member of one Jewish community that shares information under the umbrella of One Jewish Asheville (OJA). Representatives and professional leaders of the various Jewishly affiliated organizations meet monthly as The Asheville Jewish Leadership Collaborative (AJLC), formed in 2006.

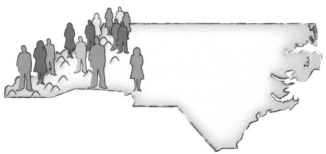

(Graphic Courtesy 2010 Western North Carolina Jewish Demographic Study)

Who is the Jewish Community?

In 2010, the AJLC engaged demographers from Brandeis University to conduct the first-ever Jewish population study of the area. The results revealed:

- 3,400 people lived in Jewish-connected homes in Western North Carolina (WNC) and at least another 835 were seasonal residents.

- 72% of the Jewish-connected households were located in Buncombe County. 13% were in Henderson County and the remainders were spread among 14 other counties in Western North Carolina (WNC).

- Nearly 60% of all Jewish-connected households in WNC moved to the area between 2000 and 2010 and nearly 80% arrived between 1990 and 2010.

- The mean age of Asheville's Jewish community was 49.3 years; an estimated 28% of the population was 65 years or older; 21% were 55-64; 21% were 35-54; 15% were 18-34; children (aged 17 or younger) made up 15% of the population. The entire report can be accessed from www.onejewishasheville.org.

Collaborations

OJA brings together community volunteers and professionals who share a common goal, such as youth education, fundraising or member engagement. These individuals represent multiple organizations and programs within the OJA community. Collaborations include: Youth Programming for kids ages 12-18, keeping them "Jewishly connected" throughout the school year. All teen programming is open to any Jewish child; they need not be a member of any organization to participate. Middle-schoolers participate in the Gesher Program and high school students can join BBYO (B'nai B'rith Youth Organization) through Kol Harim, Asheville's co-ed BBYO chapter.

What Jewish organizations participate in OJA?

OJA and the AJLC include CBHT, CBI, and the JCC, as well as the following organizations:

Agudas Israel Synagogue

505 Glasgow Lane
Hendersonville, NC 28739

Agudas Israel Synagogue founded in 1900, is a reform congregation in Hendersonville, NC affiliated with the Union for Reform Judaism (formerly UAHC).
- www.agudasisraelsynagogue.org

Asheville Jewish Business Forum (AJBF) connects Jewish and Jewish supported businesses, people and professionals, through networking dinner and luncheon meetings. Here relationships are forged that have strengthened Jewish business and community.
• www.ashevillejewishbusiness.com

ASHEVILLE JEWISH
BUSINESS FORUM

Carolina Jews for Justice (CJJ) West is a grassroots Jewish network committed to creating a just, fair and compassionate North Carolina. Founded in March 2013, CJJ combines advocacy and education to organize a non-partisan Jewish voice in North Carolina. They work to influence policy at the local and state levels and encourage individuals and Jewish institutions to take a stand on important issues in our community, including the environment, voting rights, tolerance and respect for diversity and public education, among others.
• https://carolinajews.wordpress.com/tag/west/
•https://www.facebook.com/CarolinaJewsForJustice
• wncjewsforjustice1@gmail.com

The **Center for Jewish Studies at UNC Asheville** (CJS) serves the University and the Asheville community, successfully bringing them together intellectually, artistically, and spiritually. The CJS coordinates academic course offerings in Jewish Studies, and hosts visiting lecturers and performing artists as well as encourages and supports the activities of UNC Asheville's Jewish students. The Center, through the efforts of Dr. Richard Chess, Director, collaborates with other organizations to produce the annual Jewish Film Festival. CJS has also helped to support the Jewish Life in Western North Carolina archival collection of local Jewish history at Ramsey Library Special Collections.
• http://toto.lib.unca.edu/collections/jewish_life_wnc.htm.
• www.cjs.unca.edu

Hillel at UNC Asheville is a student-led organization devoted to connecting and supporting Jewish students.
• sites.google.com/site/uncahillel/contact-informationhillel/home
• unca.hillel@gmail.com.
• Karpen Hall 208 • (828) 251-6576
• UNC Asheville Hillel on Facebook

Jewish Family Services To assist. To empower. To learn. To give. **JFS** is a non-profit agency serving the needs of individuals and families across Western North Carolina. Those seeking assistance today may be the ones to provide help for others tomorrow. Throughout the cycle of giving and receiving, JFS is there.
• www.jfswnc.org

Jewish Secular Community of Asheville (JSCA) provides a warm, inclusive and secular, humanistic environment in which to celebrate Jewish holidays, traditions and history, as well as discuss current issues throughout the year.

• http://jscasheville.org/ • president@jscasheville.org • 828-243-7815

With a love for Jewish life and an ardor for living Jewishly, **The Chabad House Asheville** provides social, educational, and religious opportunities, satisfying the hearts and minds of all. The Chabad House, a Center for Jewish Living and Learning, is open to everyone.

• www.chabadasheville.org

The WNC Jewish Federation (WNCJF) raises and distributes funds in Asheville and Western North Carolina, Israel and around the world.

• www.jewishasheville.org

Selected Bibliography

Listed here are books, articles, websites and written and electronic sources used in researching this book. The University of North Carolina-Asheville D. Hiden Ramsey Library Special Collections contains the Jewish Life in Western North Carolina Collection and is rich with historical information about Asheville and Western North Carolina. These resources also contain a large number of oral history interviews, some of which are referenced here.

Pack Memorial Library North Carolina Collection houses the JCC archives, sources on many of Asheville's businesses and oral histories of Kerry Friedman, Paul Michalove and the Marty Gillen collection recorded for the 75th anniversary of the JCC. Additional information about many of the contemporary people included here can be found by searching the web for their individual websites.

Beaver, Patricia D. African-American and Jewish Relations in Early Twentieth Century Asheville, North Carolina. Unpublished paper. Boone, NC Center for Appalachian Studies, Appalachian State University (ASU) Boone, NC. 1997.

Beaver, Patricia D. Jewish Roots in Appalachia: The Development of the Jewish Community in Asheville, North Carolina. Center for Appalachian Studies, Appalachian State University. 1997.

—1998. *Leo Finkelstein's Asheville and The Poor Man's Bank*, Patricia D. Beaver editor, Katheryn L. Staley, Associate Editor, Boone, NC. Center For Appalachian Studies, Appalachian State University..

Carol Grotner Belk Library Special Collections Appalachian State University, Leo Finkelstein collection.

Epstein, Seth. Ph.D. Candidate, "From Objects to Agents of Tolerance: Jews, Public Space, and Political Culture in Asheville, North Carolina, 1926-1950". Ph.D. dissertation. University of Minnesota, 2013.

Evans, Eli. *The Provincials: a Personal History of Jews in the South*. New York: Athenaeum. 1973.

Fahrer, Sharon. 2014 History@Hand, Jewish Museum without Walls. www.history-at-hand.com interpretive panels.

Fahrer, Sharon and Schochet, Jan, T*he Family Store, A History of Jewish Businesses in Downtown Asheville, 1880-1990*. Asheville, NC: History@Hand, 2008.

Golden, Harry. *Jewish Roots in the Carolinas A Pattern of American Philo-Semitism*. Greensboro, N.C.: Deal Print Co. 1955.

Goldring-Woldenberg Institute of Southern Jewish Life, Encyclopedia of Southern Jewish Communities, Asheville, NC. http://www.isjl.org/north-carolina-asheville-encyclopedia.html

Grossman, Rachel. "If Walls Could Speak: A Material Culture Study on Temple Beth HaTephila, Asheville, North Carolina", paper for the department of Religious Studies, UNC Asheville. 2010.

Marcus, Jacob Rader. *To Count a People: American Jewish Population Data 1585-1984*. Lanham, MD. University Press of America, Inc. 1990.

McKinney, Gordon B. Zeb Vance, North Carolina's Civil War Governor and Gilded Age Political Leader. Chapel Hill and London: The University of North Carolina Press, 2004.

Noblitt, Phillip T. *A Mansion in the Mountains The Story of Moses and Bertha Cone and Their Blowing Rock Manor*; Catawba Publishing Company 1996.

Rogoff, Leonard. *Down Home Jewish Life in North Carolina*. Chapel Hill and London: The University of North Carolina Press, 2010.

Sternberg, Jerry. *The Gospel According to Jerry*, 80th Birthday Edition Asheville, NC self-published 2010.

Weinstein, Maurice A. editor, *Zebulon Vance The Scattered Nation*. Charlotte, N.C. The Wildacres Press, 1995.

Websites:

Bayer, Bob. What to Wear, Part One and Two http://www.nonwovens-industry.com/contents/view_experts-opinion/2010-03-04/what-to-wear-part-two/#sthash.NWzycM2C.dpuf and http://www.nonwovens-industry.com/contents/view_experts-opinion/2010-02-22/what-to-wear-part-one/#sthash.21xFxdQw.dpuf

Hadley Manufacturing. Vintage Fashion Guild. http://vintagefashionguild.org/label-resource/hadley/

Interviews:

The Western North Carolina Jewish Heritage Collection, UNC Asheville. D. Hiden Ramsey Library Special Collections:

UNC Asheville Center for Jewish Studies. Interviews by David Schulman: Schocket, Sidney. 1994. (Schochet misspelled). Finkelstein, Leo.1994. Benniga, Helen. 1994. Goldstein, Sarah. 1994. Kolodkin, Ann.1994. Marder, Estelle. 1994. Lichtenfels, Joe. 1994.

Interviews by Sharon Fahrer and Jan Schochet. History@Hand: Golden, Stan. 2005. Robinson, Michael 2003. Patton, Marilyn, 2004. Lurey, Milton, 2003. Leon Rocamora, 2004.

Interviews by Leonard Rogoff for *Down Home Jewish Life in North Carolina*: Sternberg, Jerry, 2007. Julianne Winner, 2007.

Interviews by Marty Gillen for the JCC archives in the North Carolina Collection, Pack Memorial Library. 2015: Kahn, Fred; Winner, Gene; Doloboff, Jack and Arlene; Slosman, Jeff; Michalove, Ken.

Donors

Alan & Ellen Kellam

Asheville Medicine and Pediatrics

Bankers Insurance

Barbara and William Lewin

Center for Jewish Studies at UNC Asheville

Congregation Beth HaTephila

Congregation Beth Israel

Daryl Flatte and Richard David

Dennis Winner

Dr. Paul and Barbara Michalove

Hedy Fisher

Jeff and Barbara Wasserman

Jerry Dave & Barbara Shagan Dave

Joan and William Rocamora

Ken Betsalel and Heidi Kelley

Kerry and Anna Friedman

Kim and Hank Teich

Larry and Marcia Schantz

Laser Precision Cutting

McGuire, Wood & Bissette Law Firm

Patla, Straus, Robinson & Moore, P.A.

Paul and Pat Samuels

Payment Collect

Robert & Carol Deutsch

Stuart Financial Services

Van Winkle Law Firm

Vinnie's Neighborhood Italian

Index

About The Author

Sharon Fahrer was a recovering New Yorker who made Asheville her home in 1996. She and her husband, Vic were drawn to Asheville because of its sense of history. They purchased an 1896 Queen Ann Victorian house in the heart of the Montford historic district and dove into its restoration.

Sharon Fahrer (Courtesy of Laurie Johnson Photography)

Sharon co-founded History@Hand with Jan Schochet in 2003. They documented Asheville's downtown retail Jewish history, creating an exhibit and book entitled *The Family Store: A History of Jewish Businesses in Downtown Asheville from 1880-1990*. This project has encouraged families to donate material to *Jewish Life in Western North Carolina*, an archival collection at UNC Asheville's D. Hiden Ramsey Library Special Collections. They also coauthored *The Man Who Lived on Main Street*, a book about Sol Shulman, who ran a business in Sylva, North Carolina for 70 years.

Sharon went on to create the *Jewish Museum without Walls*, which has interpretive history panels at Jewish sites around Asheville and on the campus of UNC Asheville. She also leads a Jewish walking tour of downtown. It is her passion to share the wealth of history and stories, some unique and some universal, with visitors and residents alike.

Sharon earned a BA in Geography from Clark University and her Master's in Urban Planning from Wayne State University. She worked for various consulting firms as an environmental planner as well as the Southern Appalachian Mountains Initiative (SAMI). An avid volunteer, Sharon founded the Montford Music and Arts Festival in 2003 and has served on many non-profit boards in the community.

CPSIA information can be obtained
at www.ICGtesting.com
Printed in the USA
BVHW020327011221
622869BV00002B/18